Instant Loss
Quick and Easy

Also by Brittany Williams

Instant Loss Cookbook

Instant Loss: Eat Real, Lose Weight

Instant Loss on a Budget

Dear Body: What I Lost, What I Gained, and What I Learned Along the Way

Instant Loss
Quick and Easy

125 Recipes That Are Big on Flavor
When You're Light on Time

Brittany Williams
Photography by Ghazalle Badiozamani

HARVEST
An Imprint of WILLIAM MORROW

HarperCollins books may be purchased for educational, business,
or sales promotional use. For information, please email the
Special Markets Department at SPsales@harpercollins.com.

FIRST EDITION

Designed by Tai Blanche

Photography by Ghazalle Badiozamani

Chapter opener paper © arturaliev/Stock.Adobe.com

Library of Congress Cataloging-in-Publication Data has been
applied for.

ISBN 978-0-358-53990-2

24 25 26 27 28 TC 10 9 8 7 6 5 4 3 2 1

To You,

My Instant Loss Family, it's only fitting that this book be dedicated to all of you. To the friendships we've built over the last seven years. To the recipes we've cooked, to the stories we've shared, and to the life we lived all along the way. You've made an imprint on me that will last the rest of my days and I am eternally grateful to have known you. I wouldn't be here without you.

Bishop TD Jakes says, "If you can't figure out your purpose, figure out your passion. For your passion will lead you right into your purpose." I've always been a passionate individual. Learning to lean into that instead of run away from it led to the greatest adventure of my life so far.

This. You. Us.

Thank you for everything.

Contents

Introduction...1

Juices, Drinks,
and Smoothies..........47

Morning Quickies 59

Super Soups............75

Snappy Salads..........91

Simple Sides.......... 107

Meatless Mains........119

Recipes for One....... 139

One-Pot Wonders......151

5-Ingredient Meals ... 169

15-Minute Meals.......181

Casseroles, Sheet
Pans, and Skillets..... 199

Sweet Tooth 215

Make-at-Home
Money Savers 233

Acknowledgments.. 250
Index 253

Introduction

"I don't have the time." A narrative I've allowed to prevail throughout the years of my life. When life gets hard, when life gets busy, it's easy to put my well-being on the back burner. It's the path of least resistance. The path that gets me another "you're the best mom ever!" as I make a trip through the drive-thru or stop at the gas station for chips and candy. The path that leads to midnight bonding with my partner while we binge-watch TV and share a tub of ice cream and a bottle of wine. The path that leaves all my guests raving about the food I made, not because I'm a great cook, but because I know how to add cream cheese and sugar to things to get them to hit just right.

Sometimes "I don't have time" translates to "I don't have the bandwidth." Sometimes it's shorthand for "I don't want to," and sometimes I really *don't* have the time. But most often, it's a convenient excuse to get me out of doing what I need to do so that I can do what *feels* best in the moment.

Let's be honest: eating the standard American diet feels good—at least at first. More than that, I've formed attachments to consuming these ultra-processed items. I crave them when I'm sad, lonely, stressed, in good spirits, irritated, overwhelmed, celebrating, tired. It's readily available, inexpensive, and on every corner, so I get it with little to no effort, and in the moment it makes me feel so happy, happy, happy that I'm nearly able to forget the inevitable fallout.

The fallout is what I'm experiencing right now as I type this. I regained 40 pounds, my inflammation is completely out of control, with rashes, acne, puffy face, and swollen eyelids, and my thyroid numbers are so high they're not through the roof, they're on the moon.

At this moment, I have two choices: continue down the path of least resistance or *make* time.

Starting Out

As a woman who wears many hats—business owner, author, influencer, mother, teacher, wife, daughter, and friend—I have an incredibly busy schedule. I initially lost 125 pounds while my kids were young. This was all before school and friend obligations, before work deadlines, and before consulting the internet on every choice I make. When I initially started losing weight, I actually fasted from social media for a month. After I broke my fast, I made a rule that social media was only for the parts of the day when my children were sleeping. I didn't want to raise them with a phone in my face.

That social media fast was a tenfold blessing. Not only did it encourage me to get out of my house and comfort zone and make real, in-person friends, but it showed me that I really did have the time. When I eliminated screens, all of a sudden I had time to stay on top of the laundry, dishes, and household chores that I'd never had time for before. When I stopped picking up my phone to scroll, I magically had time to cook three meals a day and prepare snacks and desserts.

In 2017, I resolutely declared that I wasn't going to eat out for a year. On top of that, I decided that I was done with processed and packaged convenience foods and I was going to learn how to make convenient food at home. Over the five years that followed, I stuck with it. I truly enjoyed the new lifestyle and behavioral patterns I'd formed. For the first time in my life, I was running miles and hiking mountains, and I liked the way I looked.

There's a statistic that 80 percent of people who lose weight will have regained it all plus some by year five. I was proud to be in the 20 percent that had maintained for so long, with little holiday hiccups here and there, but maintaining overall. I had even more motivation to keep the weight off than most, as it's what I'd built a business out of. I was a beacon of hope, showing people that there wasn't a need for a pill, scheme, shot, or surgery—that none of those things will work over the long term anyway without serious lifestyle changes. And I could show everyone how. . . .

But unresolved trauma does strange things to a person, and the body always keeps score. In 2022 I wrote a very personal book called *Dear Body*. For the first time in five years, my job wasn't in the kitchen anymore, it was at the writer's desk. The toll that reliving my life's deepest traumas and heartbreaks, through the written word, had on my body was similar to the first go-round.

It resulted in tremendous weight gain. I began to loosen my grip on what my body needed to stay well in favor of what my mind told me would make me feel better in the moment. It wanted comfort and ease of living, and to go back into hiding.

I let little things back in at first. Foods I knew that I was sensitive to or that triggered me. Then I stopped hiking, I stopped running, I stopped moving, and I started to hide again. If things in motion stay in motion, then things that don't are dead.

The lie I told myself was that I was healed, and if I wasn't disordered then I could consume anything in modest portions. But that'd be like telling an alcoholic that in order to say they're sober they have to coexist with a bottle of tequila on the counter, taking shots periodically just to prove they can moderate. You see, it's acceptable to acknowledge that there are people who struggle with moderating things like alcohol. But if you struggle with food moderation and opt to abstain from certain triggers you're not practicing sobriety . . . you have an eating disorder. Those who have never struggled with addiction can't truly understand what it's like to live with a mind that constantly tells you that the poison surest to kill you is the only thing that is going to save you or make you feel better.

I cannot successfully regulate my triggers all the time. I cannot consume my food sensitivities in modest portions. My body rebels. It hates it. It screams and signals to me with things like acne, rashes, thyroid disease, iron deficiency, ferritin issues, and lymphedema that my brain is wrong. That those foods are poison. That keeping them out of my life is the only way to achieve long-term health.

Most of us know what we need to do. But overcoming ourselves, our flesh, the world . . . well, it's certainly not the path of least resistance. But it is the path to life.

You don't have time? Neither do I. So let's figure out how to make it.

K.I.S.S.

"Keep it simple stupid," words to live by really. Here's another: J.E.R.F. It means "just eat real food." If it comes from the earth, or has limited whole food ingredients, I eat it. If it's ultra-processed or made with chemicals they formulate in a lab, I avoid it. This makes shopping and meal planning fairly simple. I can already feel you trying to complicate this. Don't.

You know what real food is—fruits, vegetables, whole gains, legumes, herbs, spices, animal protein, honey, pure maple syrup—you know, that stuff that comes from trees! This isn't a diet. Diets tell you all the things you're not allowed to do. And let's get real, most diets cut out some of the most cost-effective *healthy* foods in the grocery store! Legumes, whole grains, and starchy carbohydrates—these complex, nutritionally dense foods are filling and packed full of protein and other micronutrients. They're great for the body, yet we cut them out because we're afraid of carbs! This is a lifestyle, and only you know what your body needs. We are all bio-individual, so what makes mine feel best is going to vary slightly from yours. That's why I love J.E.R.F.: it's the one-size-fits-all strategy that you self-moderate according to what you know is best for you.

For instance, some people do best on a higher-fat diet and others on a higher-carb diet—neither is wrong, as they're both just units of energy.

Consume too much and your body will store the excess for future use. Consume the right amount and your body will have just enough to get through the day without having to store any!

Portion Sizes and Counting Calories

As Sheba Smith in 1840 so succinctly put it, "As it is said, there are more ways than one to skin a cat." (I bet you never thought you'd read that in a cookbook!)

I am not a fan of calorie or macro counting. It requires a lot of extra effort and time. This is where you say, "But if you're not counting calories, how do you know how much to eat?" Well, dear friend, I use my hand to gauge correct food portions for each food group (per the Arizona State University College of Health Solutions).

Protein: It's customary to eat 3 to 4 ounces of a protein source at mealtime. A great way to judge how much you should eat is by using the palm of your hand as a portion guide. The protein portion should be the size of your palm, not including your fingers or thumb.

Vegetables: The perfect portion of a side of vegetables at mealtime is two hands cupped together.

Fruit: A good portion guide for fruit is about one cupped hand.

Starches: Clench your hand to form a fist. That's as much starchy carbohydrates as you should eat for one portion. It's ½ to 1 cup.

Fats: I'm a fan of healthy fats. It's recommended that a healthy serving of fats like peanut butter, mayo, or oil is equal to the size of your thumb. I'm a bit more indulgent than that, though, and often eat a little more.

This is a no-fuss way to gauge portion size, and it doesn't matter where I am since my hand is always with me. There is nothing wrong with calorie or macro counting, but if you're out to save time, this is truly the quickest way.

Food Matters

When I was a teenager, my mom noticed that I was rapidly gaining weight despite eating the same foods as my siblings. She scheduled a doctor's visit and, after a blood panel, I was diagnosed with hypothyroid disease. I was told that I would require a synthetic hormone supplement for the rest of my life, that I needed doctor visits every six months to adjust the dosage, and that I was high risk for thyroid cancer.

I remember feeling relieved because I finally had an explanation for the ailments that plagued me. Weight gain, profuse sweating, always too hot or too cold, irregular periods, hair loss, constipation, dry skin, brittle nails, puffy face, exhaustion—it wasn't a problem with me, it was a problem with my body, with the way that I was made. I was just sick and there was nothing that could be done about it. I didn't understand then how dangerous this line of thinking was for me. It removed all accountability.

After I had my first baby, I watched a documentary called *Fat, Sick and Nearly Dead* in which a man, Joe Cross, healed his autoimmune disease through juice fasting. It was revolutionary to me. It had never occurred to me that an autoimmune disease could be healed or that remission could be achieved. My physicians told me that once the thyroid began to produce less thyroid hormone, there was no way to get it to produce more again. Pills were the only answer.

But what if they weren't? What if my thyroid disease wasn't a disease at all? What if it was just a dysfunction caused by insufficient nourishment? What if my body, though overweight, was actually malnourished in crucial vitamins, minerals, and nutrients that it needed in order to produce adequate thyroid hormone?

Thirteen years ago, a quick Google search or trip to the library didn't yield any help in this regard, so I decided to test my theory on myself. I adopted a whole foods diet with an emphasis on plant foods. By the time my daughter turned one I had lost nearly 100 pounds and my thyroid disease was in remission.

Food matters. It is undeniable.

Holistic health practitioner Ann Wigmore once said, "The food you eat can be either the safest and most powerful form of medicine or the slowest form of poison." And yet you know the most foolish thing that we humans do? As soon as we feel better, we stop. The second that something starts working for us, we abandon it in favor of habit, convenience, and comfort, forgetting that we need it.

I wish that I could tell you the first time I lost 100 pounds was the last time, but it wasn't. I would go on to relapse over and over. I never really stopped to fix the root of my problem, which wasn't food. It was a mismanagement of emotions deeply rooted in avoidance. I think the second half of life is about learning to heal and let go of the things you collected in the first half.

Time is the only thing we never get back. It's precious, and the question of how we spend it deserves serious consideration. Food is not just for nourishment but for connection. It's a way that we can relate, show affection and love. It's a way to nourish our souls as well as our bodies. I think we've lost touch with how meaningful the preparation, care, and thought we put into our meals actually is.

As you'll find in this book, you don't need tons of time to make this happen. You can make a delicious, home-cooked meal with very little time— and I'm going to show you how.

Mealtime Madness

Mealtime used to fill me with a sense of dread. It was a deadline that I wasn't prepared for, and it was quickly approaching. I would have anxiety all day about what I was going to make for dinner. Then one afternoon I decided to set a timer. I was curious how long it actually took. I was surprised to discover that even with my kids interrupting, it took me only about 15 minutes of actual prep and work.

I started to reframe the way I thought about meal making in terms of time. Instead of this lengthy, exhausting to-do, it became an episode of *The Office*, a quick scroll session on Instagram, or four of my favorite songs. If I had time to do those things throughout the day, I absolutely had time to make dinner.

It was easy to use the excuse "I don't have the time," but honestly, I did have the time. Making dinner just wasn't important to me. We make time for the things that matter. Which is why I also had to understand why making food at home was important. I had to make it matter.

In 2017, when I first decided to make over our diets, I knew that time management was a big issue of mine. So, I put parameters on the things I found difficult to manage regarding time. I limited my TV intake to one movie or two episodes of a show. I wasn't allowed to get on social media unless it was my kids' naptime. If I wanted to talk for a lengthy amount of time on the phone with a friend, I had to do chores or take a walk while talking.

I have to tell you, I was amazed to discover just how much time I actually had that was being squandered meaninglessly throughout the day. My house had never been cleaner, my mind never clearer, and a lifestyle change never so easy to stick to. Not only had TV and social media become massive time sucks, but worse, they'd become energy sucks. The news, disasters, and constant barrage of information bogged me down and weighed heavily on me throughout the day. I hadn't even realized how much this was the case until I went without it and regained my energy, creativity, and, quite frankly, joy.

Keep-It-Quick Tips

I love that eating well is becoming mainstream. No longer are we limited to pricey health food stores! Even Walmart has jumped on board, creating gluten-free and dairy-free sections as well as quick premade meals and ingredients. Here are some tips that can help you make eating well easier.

- Watch YouTube videos on the most efficient way to chop vegetables. Make sure you keep your knives sharpened. Prep is the bulk of the time any cook spends in the kitchen. Making sure you have the proper utensils and know the proper techniques is key to avoiding frustration and increasing productivity.

- Work when you have time. If you have extra time on Sundays, in the morning, or while your kids are napping, chop up all your vegetables for the week. Then, later in the week when you don't have as much time, all you have to do is grab your prepped veggies and cook. This requires a little bit of forethought, but depending on your schedule, it can really help minimize the mental weight of creating meals.

- Lean on freezer meals. Did you know that virtually any meal can become a freezer meal? Simply add vegetables, protein, spices, and sauces to a ziplock bag and place in the freezer. Then, when you're ready to eat that meal, all you have to do is dump and cook! My magic number for frozen meals with chicken is 30 minutes in the electric pressure cooker. If the meal calls for ground beef, I recommend cooking the beef before freezing it.

- K.I.S.S.—keep it simple stupid. When all else fails, keep it simple. Two veggies. One protein. One complex carb. Use whatever you have on hand. If it's eggs, make eggs and toast with roasted asparagus and peppers. Don't know how? Just google "how to roast asparagus with peppers." You can do this with anything you have on hand. "How to roast chicken breast with vegetables." "How to make frozen shrimp in the air fryer." We literally have the answers to every question imaginable, in our pockets, at all times. You can also see pages 13 to 14 for some great starter recipes.

- Set a timer. I love to race against the clock. I do this often on Instagram, where I'll make an entire meal while filming a video for y'all and show you the amount of time it took to complete it. It usually ranges from

5 to 25 minutes. It reminds me that it really doesn't require as much time as I think it does, and it encourages you guys to get up and get cooking.

- Find meals that your family loves and put them in the rotation. Part of feeling like we don't have the time is actually the weight of making decisions and trying to please everyone. Take note when your family likes something and then assign that meal to a day of the week to eliminate the mental fatigue of making decisions! Here, I'll help! Mondays = Meatless, Tuesdays = Tacos, Wednesdays = Salads, Thursdays = Soup or Stew, Friday = Pizza Night, Saturday = Eat out, Sunday = Sunday dinner.

- Freeze soups in silicone molds so they're the perfect serving size for lunches. Souper Cubes makes some great and easy-to-use molds.

- Double the recipe! If it's something you know that everyone likes, make twice as much so you have leftovers for meals throughout the week, or freeze half for later.

Simple, Easy, Cheap

If you are making the lifestyle adjustment to eating well, it's best to keep things simple. I'll be honest, most of the meals made in my home are cobbled together with odds, ends, and leftovers. Roast a chicken breast, make a large salad, steam some sweet potatoes, and season them to taste.

I think we psych ourselves out a lot. We assume that taking care of ourselves requires a lot of time, energy, and know-how, but it really doesn't. The truth is that it's mostly intuitive. Your body knows what it needs. You already know the best way to feed yourself. The key is accessing the information and applying it in sustainable ways. Part of that is making it as easy on yourself as possible.

Pick one thing to make each day and find some simple, easy staples for the other two meals. Remember, you don't have to eat breakfast for breakfast! I can't tell you how many times we've eaten scrambled eggs, toast, and bacon for dinner, or last night's dinner leftovers for breakfast!

When in doubt, J.E.R.F.: just eat real food. It's really that simple.

Here are eight of my favorite things to throw together on the fly that require hardly any prep time at all!

Chicken Salad

8 ounces cooked chicken, chopped
   or shredded

½ cup diced celery

½ cup quartered purple grapes

¼ cup chopped pecans, walnuts,
   or sunflower seeds

¼ cup mayonnaise, homemade (page 240)
   or store-bought

1 teaspoon dried dillweed

¼ teaspoon fine sea salt

⅛ teaspoon ground black pepper

Combine all of the ingredients in
a medium bowl. Serve over rice cakes
or salad, or in romaine lettuce leaves.

Egg Salad

Serves 2

4 hard-boiled eggs (see page 22),
   peeled and chopped or mashed

1 tablespoon mustard

1½ tablespoons mayonnaise, homemade
   (page 240) or store-bought

¼ cup diced dill pickles

¼ teaspoon apple cider vinegar

⅛ teaspoon paprika

⅛ teaspoon fine sea salt

⅛ teaspoon ground black pepper

Combine all of the ingredients in
a medium bowl. Serve over rice cakes
or salad, or in romaine lettuce leaves.

Tuna Salad

Serves 2

1 (5-ounce) can wild-caught tuna, drained

¼ cup mayonnaise, homemade (page 240)
   or store-bought

¼ cup sweet relish

Fine sea salt, to taste

Ground black pepper, to taste

Combine all of the ingredients in
a medium bowl. Serve over rice cakes
or salad, or in romaine lettuce leaves.

Vegetable Platter with Ranch

Any cut-up vegetables and fruit you need
   to get rid of

Hard-boiled eggs (see page 22),
   peeled and cut in half

Sliced or cubed cheese

Sliced deli meat

Nuts and/or seeds

1 recipe ranch dressing, homemade
   (page 153) or store-bought

Arrange all of the dippers on a large
platter and put a bowl of ranch dressing
in the center.

Eggs, Bacon, and Toast

('nough said, no recipe needed)

Popcorn and Smoothies

Home-popped popcorn with sea salt and
   avocado oil, coconut oil, grass-fed butter,
   or ghee

Your favorite smoothie

Simple Salad

Mixed greens plus any cut-up vegetables
or fruits you need to get rid of

Extra-virgin olive oil

Balsamic vinegar, apple cider vinegar,
red wine vinegar, Dijon mustard,
or horseradish

Fine sea salt, to taste

Ground black pepper, to taste

Combine all of the ingredients in a
medium bowl. Serve immediately. For
a sweeter dressing, add a drizzle of honey
or pure maple syrup.

PB&J Rice Cake

Serves 1

1 lightly salted brown rice cake

Nut or seed butter of choice

Low-sugar jelly

Spread the rice cake with the nut butter
and jelly. Enjoy with a side of veggie sticks
(carrots, cucumbers, celery, bell peppers).

Grab On-the-Go

Fruits

Apples

Clementines

Dried fruit

Frozen berries

Applesauce

Bananas

Watermelon

Pineapple

Grapes

Grapefruit

Vegetables

Celery

Broccoli

Edamame

Bell peppers

Cherry tomatoes

Carrots

Cucumbers

Small salad

Sweet potato fries

Miscellaneous

Beef or turkey sticks
(I like Paleovalley
brand)

Hard-boiled eggs
(see page 22)

Corn tortilla chips

Create-your-own
trail mix

Popcorn

Nuts

Rice cakes

Banana chips

Apple chips

Muffins

Smoothie or juice

Plantain chips

Nitrate- and sugar-
free deli meat

Dill pickles

Dips

Hummus

Ranch dressing,
homemade
(page 153) or
store-bought

Avocado with lime
juice, fine sea salt,
and garlic powder

Nut or seed butter

Homemade FTW!

There are certain things that are just more cost-effective to make at home. When purchasing things like broth and nondairy milk, it's best to keep your money in your pocket and simply make them from scratch!

In the Make-at-Home Money Savers chapter, you can find my favorite recipes for Homemade Bone Broth (page 243) and Vegetable Broth (page 244).

If you are dairy-free or purchasing a lot of raw or organic milk, things can add up quickly! For this reason, my absolute favorite, cost-effective milk to use in my recipes is oat milk. It's very simple to throw together. Simply toss 1 cup old-fashioned rolled oats and 4 cups ice-cold water into a blender. Blend on high for no more than 20 seconds, then strain the mixture through a nut milk bag. It's important not to overblend the oat milk because you can begin to unintentionally heat the oats and turn them gummy.

Another concern with oat milk is that it has a tendency to become a bit slimy from the starch content. Amylase is a digestive enzyme that helps break down starch. If you find that your oat milk is yielding slimy results, try soaking 1 cup old-fashioned rolled oats in 2 cups water with 2 digestive enzymes capsules (powder only, outside capsules discarded) for 15 minutes. Drain and rinse the oats and proceed with the recipe. (This is a tip I learned from Downshiftology.)

The same process can be used with raw almonds, raw cashews, hemp seeds, or unsweetened shredded coconut in lieu of the rolled oats. Already blended nuts are an option if you don't have a high-powered blender. See page 234 for my Almond Butter Almond Milk recipe! The following table details the preparation of each milk. Add a splash of pure vanilla extract and a tablespoon of pure maple syrup if you'd like a lightly sweetened vanilla milk.

Base	Cold Water	Blend	Strain	Store
1 cup old-fashioned rolled oats	4 cups water	20 seconds on high	Nut milk bag, squeeze gently	Glass container in the refrigerator for up to 1 week
1 cup raw almonds	4 cups water	60 seconds on high	Nut milk bag or cheesecloth, wring as hard as you can	Glass container in the refrigerator for up to 5 days
1 cup raw cashews	4 cups water	40 seconds on high	Nut milk bag, squeeze gently	Glass container in the refrigerator for up to 5 days
1 cup hulled hemp seeds or hearts	4 cups water	40 seconds on high	Nut milk bag, squeeze gently	Glass container in the refrigerator for up to 1 week
1 cup unsweetened shredded coconut	4 cups water	40 seconds on high	Nut milk bag, squeeze gently	Glass container in the refrigerator for up to 1 week

Electric Pressure Cooker Cook Time Cheat Sheet

Meats

Water ratios:

6-quart pressure cooker: 1 cup water or broth

8-quart pressure cooker: 1½ cups water or broth

Whole chicken (3 pounds) 25 minutes / High pressure / Natural release

Note: Add 6 minutes for each additional pound of chicken.

Chicken breasts, **whole or cubed** (1 pound) 6 minutes / High pressure / Natural release

Chicken drumsticks (1 pound) 10 minutes / High pressure / Natural release

Ground beef (1 pound) 5 to 8 minutes / Sauté / Normal

Beef roast (3 to 4 pounds) 90 minutes / High pressure / Natural release

Stew meat (1-inch pieces, 1 to 2 pounds) 35 minutes / High pressure / Natural release

Ribs 25 minutes / High pressure / Natural release

Pork loin or rump roast (2 to 3 pounds) 60 minutes / High pressure / Natural release

Fish fillet 2 to 3 minutes / High pressure / Natural release

Mussels 1 to 2 minutes / High pressure / Natural release

Beans

Water ratios unsoaked: 1 cup beans to 3 cups water or broth

Water ratios soaked: 1 cup beans to 2 cups water or broth

Black beans 22 minutes soaked, 50 minutes unsoaked / High pressure / Natural release

Pinto beans 25 minutes soaked, 50 minutes unsoaked / High pressure / Natural release

Cannellini beans 22 minutes soaked, 50 minutes unsoaked / High pressure / Natural release

Navy beans 20 minutes soaked, 45 minutes unsoaked / High pressure / Natural release

Kidney beans 25 minutes soaked, 50 minutes unsoaked / High pressure / Natural release

Chickpeas 25 minutes soaked, 50 minutes unsoaked / High pressure / Natural release

Lima beans 10 minutes soaked, 14 minutes unsoaked / High pressure / Natural release

Black-eyed peas 10 minutes soaked, 38 minutes unsoaked / High pressure / Natural release

Brown lentils 10 minutes unsoaked / High pressure / Natural release

Vegetables

6-quart pressure cooker: 1 cup water or broth

8-quart pressure cooker: 1½ cups water or broth

Whole potatoes (small / medium / large) 15 / 18 / 20 minutes / High pressure / Natural release

Cubed potatoes 8 minutes / High pressure / Natural release

Carrots (1-inch pieces) 3 minutes / High pressure / Quick release

Corn on the cob 2 minutes / High pressure / Quick release

Cauliflower head 2 minutes / High pressure / Quick release

Broccoli florets 1 minute / Low pressure / Quick release

Collard greens 10 minutes / High pressure / Quick release

Green beans 2 minutes / High pressure / Quick release

Brussels sprouts 2 minutes / High pressure / Quick release

Asparagus 1 to 2 minutes / Low pressure / Quick release

Butternut squash halves 4 to 6 minutes / High pressure / Quick release

Cabbage wedges 2 minutes / High pressure / Quick release

Rice and Grains

Water ratios: 1 cup rice/grain to 1½ cups water or broth

Brown rice 28 minutes / High pressure / Quick release

Basmati rice 8 minutes / High pressure / Quick release

White rice 10 minutes / High pressure / Quick release

Jasmine rice 10 minutes / High pressure / Quick release

Wild rice 28 minutes / High pressure / Quick release

Quinoa 1 minute / High pressure / 10-minute Natural release

Steel-cut oats 10 minutes / Manual high pressure / Quick release

Old-fashioned rolled oats 8 minutes / Manual high pressure / Quick release

Brown rice, quinoa, or corn pasta 6 minutes / Manual high pressure / Quick release

Miscellaneous

Hard-boiled eggs (1 dozen) 5 minutes / High pressure / 5-minute Natural release / 5-minute ice bath

Meal Plans

Planning

I've found that organizing our meals into a meal plan allows me to be more efficient with my time and mindful of what we're going to eat that day. Even if we don't eat exactly what I had planned, I always have a week's worth of breakfast, lunch, and dinner ingredients on hand so I'm never left wondering what I should make.

The vast majority of the recipes in this book use the same ingredients, repurposed in different ways. This ensures that with just a few staple ingredients, you'll be able to make several different recipes, and it virtually eliminates food waste.

On the next few pages you'll find a four-week meal plan that I hope helps you get organized! You don't have to follow these weekly meal plans strictly. They're just a guide to show you what several weeks' worth of meals might look like for me and how I'd prep accordingly.

These are only six-day meal plans because, inevitably, there will be days when you have leftovers, are on the go, or just flat-out don't feel like making what's on the meal plan. There will also be other things you'll need to purchase at the store, things for kids' lunches, the random odds and ends. These plans have been designed to get you as close as possible to under $100 a week total.

Note: For potatoes, onions, peppers, broth, and so on, colors and flavors are all interchangeable for one another. As you work through these meal plans, feel free to swap one ingredient for another if you prefer or already have something on hand.

Note 2: All of these meals are interchangeable. Just be mindful not to consume two heavier meals in one day, like pasta, rice, or bean dishes. Make this plan work for you!

4-Week Meal Plan

Week 1

	Day 1	Day 2	Day 3
Breakfast	Dried Fig and Pecan Oatmeal (page 67)	Tropical Greens (page 50) OPTIONAL: Serve with 2 eggs.	Strawberry Shortcake Smoothie (page 52) OPTIONAL: Serve with 2 eggs.
Lunch	Summertime Veggie Salad with Lemon Tahini Dressing (page 96)	Pepperoni Zucchini Pizza (page 141)	Mediterranean Herb and Bean Salad (page 94)
Dinner	The Best-Ever Cabbage Soup (page 126)	Hamburger Tacos (page 213)	Barbecue Chicken Sandwiches (page 158)

Week 2

	Day 1	Day 2	Day 3
Breakfast	Chocolate Peanut Butter Baked Oats (page 72)	Meal Replacement Smoothie (page 55) OPTIONAL: Serve with 2 eggs.	The Best Darn Green Juice (page 49) OPTIONAL: Serve with 2 eggs.
Lunch	Classic Caesar Salad (page 103)	Greek Lemon-Dill Chicken Soup (page 77)	Zesty Herby Corn and Cucumber Salad (page 142)
Dinner	Coconut Red Lentil Dal with Spinach served with brown rice (page 124)	Bang Bang Beef Lettuce Cups (page 155)	Broccoli Chicken Alfredo (page 191)

	Day 4	Day 5	Day 6
Breakfast	Red Chile Tostada (page 140)	Old-Fashioned Lemon Berry Skillet Cake (page 64)	Easy Egg Bite Casserole (page 201)
Lunch	Oven-Baked Chicken Schnitzel with Fries (page 206)	Bang Bang Beef Lettuce Cups (page 155)	Citrus Chicken Salad (page 92)
Dinner	3-Bean Turkey Chili (page 160)	Spaghetti Squash Lasagna Casserole (page 203)	Beefy Enchilada Skillet (page 210)

	Day 4	Day 5	Day 6
Breakfast	Blueberry Chia Seed Muffins (page 68)	Sweet Potato Frittata (page 71)	Southern Shrimp and Cauliflower Grits (page 62)
Lunch	Edamame Pesto Rotini (page 120)	Carrot Dogs (page 133)	Chicken Enchilada Roll-Ups (page 182)
Dinner	Jalapeño Popper Chicken Chili (page 84)	Teriyaki Salmon Rice Bowls (page 146)	Easy Chicken Ramen (page 193)

4-Week Meal Plan

Week 3

	Day 1	Day 2	Day 3
Breakfast	Creamy Peach-Orange Smoothie (page 51) OPTIONAL: Serve with 2 eggs.	The Best Pancakes Ever (page 66)	Citrus Fruit Cooler (page 55) OPTIONAL: Serve with 2 eggs.
Lunch	Roasted Eggplant with Lemon-Dill Tahini and Paprika Vinaigrette (page 123)	Pick-Up Garlicky Herb Shrimp with Creamy Cocktail Sauce (page 189)	Philly Steak Stir-Fry (page 163)
Dinner	Sesame Peanut Noodles with Edamame and Greens (page 136)	Deconstructed Stuffed Pepper Bowls (page 183)	Simple Chicken Sausage Sheet Pan (page 205)

Week 4

	Day 1	Day 2	Day 3
Breakfast	Sweet Potato Frittata (page 71)	Dried Fig and Pecan Oatmeal (page 67)	The Best Darn Green Juice (page 49) OPTIONAL: Serve with 2 eggs.
Lunch	Pumpkin Bisque (page 82)	Buffalo Chicken Wraps (page 176)	Bean and Rice Burritos (page 137)
Dinner	Penne Pasta Marinara (page 170)	Taco Chicken (page 176)	Turkey Parm Meatloaf Minis (page 161)

	Day 4	Day 5	Day 6
Breakfast	Simple Chicken Sausage Sheet Pan (page 205)	The Best Darn Green Juice (page 49) OPTIONAL: Serve with 2 eggs.	The Best Gluten-Free Banana Bread (page 60)
Lunch	Thai-Style Peanut Chicken Salad (page 105)	Herby Mango Chicken Salad (page 95)	Blueberry Kale Spring Green Salad (page 98)
Dinner	Green Chile Chicken Enchiladas (page 200)	Egg Roll in a Bowl with Sriracha Mayo (page 196)	Italian Wedding Soup (page 89)

	Day 4	Day 5	Day 6
Breakfast	Meal Replacement Smoothie (page 55) OPTIONAL: Serve with 2 eggs.	Easy Egg Bite Casserole (page 201)	Blueberry Chia Seed Muffins (page 68)
Lunch	Cobb Salad with Chicken Strips and Honey Mustard (page 101)	Chicken Pot Pie Soup (page 87)	Classic Tuna Melts (page 179)
Dinner	One-Pot Air-Fryer Salmon and Potatoes (page 174)	Sheet Pan Fajitas (page 208)	Swedish Meatballs served with mashed potatoes (page 195)

Ingredients

There may be some ingredients in this book that you are unfamiliar with. As my family began to make over our mindsets concerning food, our pantry also had a makeover. Use this as a guide to better understand why I use the ingredients I use and what substitutions you can make if you have an allergy or don't have a particular ingredient on hand!

Please note that all the recipes in this book were tested with the ingredients listed in the recipe. If you make a substitution that isn't suggested, you may end up with a different result than intended.

Eggs

All of the recipes in this book call for large eggs. I prefer to buy free-range or pasture-raised organic eggs that are certified humane and antibiotic-free. I like the Kirkland organic brand. Costco has partnered with small farms throughout the country to ensure that their hens are treated well and that they provide quality eggs.

With egg allergies becoming more prevalent, I made sure to test the baked goods in this book with egg substitutes. The two egg substitutes I've found that work the best are flax egg and aquafaba.

To make a flax egg, stir together 1 tablespoon ground flax seed and 3 tablespoons water. Let sit for 5 to 10 minutes, or until gelatinous. This makes enough to replace 1 large egg.

Aquafaba is the cooking liquid leftover when you make legumes. Chickpeas are highly recommended and the only source of aquafaba tested in these recipes. It has a slight yellow tinge to it and an egg-white/jelly-like texture. You can use the liquid from canned or home-cooked chickpeas. Use 3 tablespoons aquafaba to replace 1 large egg.

Fats

Fat has gotten a bad rap throughout the years. Much like carbohydrates, it's an energy source that the body relies on to function properly. Our cell structure needs healthy fats to thrive! My recipes call for fats that are full

of heart-healthy micronutrients that help keep our cell membranes strong. Healthy fats help boost your nutrient absorption and are essential for healthy living!

I prefer to use these organic, minimally processed fats in my cooking: extra-virgin olive oil, avocado oil, and extra-virgin coconut oil. These oils can usually be used interchangeably. When a recipe calls for a specific oil, it's because that is the oil that tastes the best in that recipe.

Flours

I am a big fan of alternative flours. Most of our traditional wheat here in the US is fortified and enriched with folic acid, the oxidized form of folate. Unfortunately, my family has a difficult time processing it because of a common gene mutation we all share. (To learn more, visit InstantLoss.com/Lets-Talk-MTHFR.) For this reason, we use alternative flours in most of our cooking, and all of the recipes in this book are gluten-free.

If you do not have a gluten sensitivity, all-purpose or whole wheat flour is absolutely healthy to consume in modest portions! Just be mindful, as wheat can be inflammatory and it is not an adequate 1:1 substitution for any of the recipes in this book.

Note: These alternative flours can be tricky to substitute, so I highly recommend using the flours suggested in the recipes.

Almond Flour

Using a blanched, superfine grind of almond flour will yield the best results for baked goods. This flour is best stored in the freezer because it can go rancid quickly. If you have a nut allergy, you can substitute ½ cup cassava flour for every 1 cup almond flour.

This can be a pricey flour, so I highly recommend purchasing it at your local big box store like Costco or shopping online sales.

Chickpea Flour

This flour is packed full of protein and relatively low in carbohydrates. It's also inexpensive! If you cannot consume legumes, you can substitute 1¼ cups superfine blanched almond flour for every 1 cup chickpea flour.

Arrowroot Powder

Arrowroot powder, also known as arrowroot flour, helps give baked goods elasticity. It's also a marvelous thickener that can be used in place of cornstarch. If you do not have arrowroot powder on hand, you can substitute tapioca starch or cornstarch 1:1 for arrowroot powder.

Coconut Flour

Super absorbent, a little bit of coconut flour goes a long, long way. Because of its unique properties, substituting it in large quantities is not recommended unless you're looking for a science experiment! If you have a coconut allergy, you can substitute ¼ cup arrowroot powder for every 1 tablespoon coconut flour.

Oat Flour

All oats are gluten-free, but not all of them are processed in a gluten-free facility. If you have celiac disease, be mindful and make sure you purchase oats with a gluten-free label to ensure there is no cross-contamination. I make my oat flour at home in a high-powered blender: 1 cup old-fashioned rolled oats yields 1 cup oat flour.

Cassava Flour

Rich in minerals like calcium, potassium, magnesium, and iron, cassava flour is made from the whole root of the yucca plant and is nonallergenic. This grain-free flour can be a little hard to find, so I order mine through Amazon. If you're not gluten-free, this flour can be substituted 1:1 with whole wheat flour.

Unfortified Nutritional Yeast

Highly nutritious, nutritional yeast is an excellent source of vitamin B_6 and contains 8 grams of protein per 2-tablespoon serving. It's a cheesy-tasting powder that's dairy-free. I use it in recipes to give a big cheesy boost. You can also sprinkle it on home-popped popcorn with sea salt and coconut oil for a delicious snack or top soups and salads with it.

This ingredient cannot be replaced with active dry yeast (the kind used for baking). It's a deactivated strain of yeast that looks like yellow flakes or powder. I purchase mine on Amazon from Sari Foods Company. One bag will last you quite a while!

Sweeteners

Maple Syrup

One hundred percent maple syrup is not the same thing as pancake syrup. Pure maple syrup is made from the sap of maple trees. It is then boiled and reduced, getting rid of some of the water content and concentrating the sweetness. Pancake syrup is usually made from corn syrup or high-fructose corn syrup and uses artificial flavorings to make it taste more like maple syrup. Pure maple syrup is a pricey ingredient, and it's sometimes tempting to substitute a cheap alternative, but in this case, you really do get what you pay for! Look for pure maple syrup that does not have any added ingredients.

Buying this ingredient in bulk at Costco saves me a bundle. If you still can't bite the bullet, you can replace this ingredient 1:1 with raw honey or, as a last resort, agave nectar.

Coconut Sugar

Also known as palm sugar, this dark, coarse sweetener is made from the sap of flower buds from the coconut palm tree. It's a fabulous brown sugar substitute. You can substitute 1:1 with raw organic cane sugar.

Raw Honey

Most of the honey that you encounter in the grocery store is made with artificial sugars, like corn syrup, and has little honey, if any, in it. It's always best to find a local source of raw honey. Local honey is a great way to battle seasonal allergies, but if you can't source it locally, any raw, organic honey will do.

Let Me Save You Some Time

Ever wonder what all the fancy buzzwords in the grocery store mean but don't have time to research it yourself? Well, I did all the legwork for you and posted the meanings below.

I don't know that you can discuss eating well without at least touching on conventional versus organic. You can absolutely eat conventionally raised/grown meat and produce and still be healthy and/or lose weight. However, it's important to know the differences between organically/conventionally grown/raised produce and meat. This can give you an understanding of why someone might opt to purchase one over the other. It does not always boil down to cost but can sometimes boil down to ethics, overall health, and well-being.

It is very important to me to purchase beef, fish, chicken, and eggs that are ethically and sustainably sourced, which can get pricey fast. It was difficult to adjust to paying higher prices for grass-fed, pasture-raised, wild-caught, and organic. I didn't convert 100% originally. Even now, I am not 100% organic.

Sometimes we have to think about things in terms of better, not best. Take it one step at a time. It's difficult to overhaul your entire diet and way of thinking in an instant. So, don't. Absorb what resonates with you and leave the rest.

Without further ado . . .

What Do These Buzzwords Mean?

GMO: Stands for genetically modified organism. It's suspected that consuming GMOs in large quantities can lead to infertility, gluten disorders, allergies, and even cancer.

Organic: When a food is labeled 100% organic, it means the food you are consuming hasn't been treated with synthetic pesticides or insecticides. It has been grown without the use of synthetic fertilizers, sewage sludge, or ionizing radiation and doesn't contain GMOs.

This is important because when you consume conventional produce, you could be taking in up to thirty different types of pesticides. These are then metabolized by your body and stored in your colon. These chemicals can harm the nervous system,

the reproductive system, and the endocrine system. People who consume more pesticides are more likely to develop cancer, Alzheimer's disease, and ADHD, and to have children with birth defects.

The Dirty Dozen and the Clean 15: If you cannot afford to purchase all organic produce (I can't either), I'd encourage you to consult the Environmental Working Group website, which puts out updated lists every year. They list the 12 "dirtiest" and the 15 "cleanest" fruits and vegetables in the food industry. The "dirtiest" foods are those grown with the most chemicals applied. The "cleanest" foods are those grown with the least or no chemicals applied. I loosely follow these guides and forgive myself the rest.

Ethically Raised: A process dedicated to promoting free-range, cruelty-free, and organic animal farming.

Sustainably Sourced: Ingredients, whether agricultural produce or meat, that are sustainably farmed with more economic considerations. Sustainable farmers take into account the environmental and social impact of their farming activities.

Certified Humane: Meat, chicken, pork, eggs, pet food, and dairy products that come from farms where the standards for the humane treatment of farm animals are being met and implemented.

Beef

Grass-Fed: This means the cattle were allowed to forage on their own for fresh food. They are sometimes supplemented with very close substitutes like alfalfa during the winter. Unlike conventionally raised grain-fed animals, they have a much more natural diet.

Grass-Finished: This means the cattle received a grass or forage diet their entire lives. It differs from grass-fed because it means they were never supplemented with grain feed.

Hormone-Free: Animals raised without additional hormones.

Antibiotic-Free: Animals raised without antibiotics in their feed or water or by injection.

Chicken and Eggs

Free-Range: This typically refers to chickens that are allowed to have freedom of movement while being kept in natural conditions.

Organic: According to the USDA, this means that the hens are "uncaged and free to roam in their houses and have access to the outdoors. The hens are fed an organic diet of feed produced without conventional pesticides or fertilizers."

Pasture-Raised: This is an unregulated term, but it typically means that chickens have plenty of time to forage and play outside. According to Mother Earth News, they have one-third less cholesterol than conventionally raised hens, one-quarter less saturated fat, two-thirds more vitamin A, twice as many omega-3 fatty acids, three times as much vitamin E, and seven times the amount of beta-carotene.

Fish

Farm-Raised: Fish that are raised in tanks, irrigation ditches, and ponds. This is not ideal because fish raised in tanks are usually plagued with disease and parasites as a result of poor water quality and a stressful environment. They can contain industrial chemicals like terephthalic acid and polyvinyl chloride, and other chemicals used to enhance their coloring. Just as we are careful about sourcing meat and chicken from sources that do not use antibiotics, we should be aware that farm-raised fish also receive antibiotics.

Farmed fish are usually grown in nets that are overcrowded. They are grown as a monoculture, or one species of fish, and can become infested with sea lice due to their congested living situation. They are usually fed an unvaried diet and are not as nutritionally rich as wild-caught fish.

Wild-Caught: Fish that come from seas, rivers, and other natural bodies of water. They have the ability to roam and eat whatever they want and are therefore more nutritious as a result of their own varied diet. They usually are lower in calories than farmed fish and have high levels of essential vitamins like potassium, zinc, and iron.

You don't have to worry about antibiotics, chemicals, or fake coloring in wild-caught fish. They also just taste better and are more humanely sourced than farm-raised fish.

Sustainably Sourced: Seafood that is caught or farmed in ways that consider the long-term vitality of harvested species and the well-being of the ocean, as well as the livelihoods of fisheries-dependent communities.

Kitchen Tools

My kitchen didn't come together overnight. I've acquired all of my kitchen gadgets and tools over the last ten years as my family's budget permitted. Investing in your kitchen by having the proper equipment will enable you to work faster and more efficiently. Being able to make many more ingredients from home will end up saving you more money in the long run and drastically reducing the time you spend inside the kitchen.

The top two things I'd advise that you invest in first are an electric pressure cooker and a high-powered blender.

Electric Pressure Cooker: All of the recipes in this book were tested with the 6-quart Instant Pot 7-in-1 Duo. I have several different electric pressure cookers and this is by far the brand and model that I love best. If you are using an 8-quart electric pressure cooker, you will need to adjust the recipes according to the manufacturer's specifications, specifically the liquids. This might require you to double some of the recipes.

Blender: Some of the recipes in this book call for a blender. Brady grew up with a Vitamix, so we pinched pennies and used birthday money to invest in one ten years ago. It was one of the best kitchen investments we've ever made. It makes it easy to make our own flours and nut/seed milks at home, and we even grind our own spices!

However, I realize that the Vitamix is not very budget-friendly, so I also tested all of the recipes in this book with a Magic Bullet. You can get one for as little as $30 at Costco or Walmart. These little powerhouses are small, compact, and get the job done.

Immersion Blender: This is a super budget-friendly kitchen gadget. Typically for $20 or $30, you can get a machine that will make pureeing soups, dressings, mayo, and more an absolute breeze.

Air Fryer: All of the air fryer recipes in this book were tested with the 5.3-quart Power AirFryer XL. Results with other air fryer brands may vary.

Juicer: Trust me when I say you do not need a $200 juicer to make amazing, fresh-squeezed juice! I have been through my fair share of juicers, and the best I've ever had, not to mention the easiest to clean, is my Jocuu Slow Masticating Juicer. It was $70 on Amazon, and it works great! I've owned $500 juicers that didn't work nearly as well and weren't as easy to clean. Save yourself some time and money and learn from my mistakes.

Stand/Hand Mixer: Many people already have a mixer as a staple tool in their kitchen, but if you don't, you can't go wrong with a KitchenAid stand mixer. The brand has amazing sales, especially around the holidays. I bought mine on clearance at Target, years ago. It was a returned item, and I snagged it for $99! Plus I was in Montana at the time, where there is no state sales tax—double score. I even treated the mixer as a carry-on item and walked right onto the plane with it. Although I got a few strange looks, it was worth it. I get, though, that a stand mixer isn't in the budget for everyone. In that case, a $20 hand mixer will do. And you can find one on the real cheap at a thrift store!

Food Processor: You don't need a big ole to-do. For $40, I bought a 10-cup Hamilton Beach 70760 on Amazon. This machine is something that makes chopping veggies, grating cheese, and blending things that are hard to dig out of a blender, like doughs and hummus, a breeze! If you can't afford one right now, that's okay. Having a food processor is not a requirement for this book, just something nice to have.

Knives: I love cheap knives! A pack of Cuisinart knives at Costco for $12? That's my jam! Last year I invested in a couple really good knives and was sad to realize that they dulled just as quickly as my cheapies. Now we make it a habit to buy new cheap knives every few years when they are really beat up. In between, Brady keeps them sharp with a manual sharpener. Just don't try to chop with dull ones, as it's an exercise in frustration.

Baking Sheets: I used rimmed stainless steel baking sheets for the recipes in this book. If you use dark-bottom pans, your results may vary.

Pots and Pans: I stick with stainless steel or cast-iron pans for all of my cooking. Some of these pieces are an investment.

Your ideal kitchen will not come together overnight. It's been ten years and I'm still building mine. Use what you have, and upgrade when you can.

Why I Don't List Nutrition Information

There are several reasons why I do not list nutritional information, the first being the negative effects that viewing food as numbers can have on an individual. I spent years tracking calories, carbs, points, and macros. For me, tracking never led to sustainable long-term success because tracking itself was not sustainable.

It also tended to put me in "diet mode." Initially my focus was to try to fit as much crummy food into my number goals as possible. My focus was not on actual nourishment or nutrition but on getting the number correct while continuing to consume food that was of poor quality. It tends to disconnect one from the body's natural hunger cues and satiety signals.

I knew that I needed to find a different way to regulate portions. I had to retrain my brain. I had to stop thinking about food as numbers and begin to think about it as fuel.

The second, probably more important reason is that depending on the brand, nutritional info can vary greatly. If you need to track nutritional info because you have a medical condition, it's best to calculate it yourself with your own ingredients.

A Word

I think we're all naturally inclined to try to keep up with the Joneses in one way or another. This has become even more apparent with influencer culture, face filters, and AI. The beauty standard has never been more difficult to achieve. And as we become more beauty-focused, it's easy to become less health-focused, inside and out. Kim Kardashian said, in 2022, that she would do anything to look younger, even if it meant eating poop every day. *Poop!*

The bar has been set impossibly high. As women, we aren't allowed to gain weight or lose it. We aren't allowed to have lines or age. We are too much, never enough, and always expected to be everything to everyone all at once.

The beauty industry generates over $100 billion in revenue worldwide every year, coming in second only to the diet industry, which is estimated to generate $405.4 billion worldwide by 2030. They set the bar so high that no one could ever possibly achieve it, and then capitalize off our greatest insecurities, the insecurities of their own making.

So let me tell you the truth:

Everything that you need is already inside you. Everything to aid in your wellness is already here, and you don't need a cream or a shot (or poop!) to transform into the person you've always dreamed of being.

You just need a little know-how, a little patience, and a little time.

So let's begin . . . again.

Juices, Drinks, and Smoothies

The Best Darn Green
   Juice 49

Tropical Greens 50

Sangria Smoothie. 50

Creamy Peach-Orange
   Smoothie. 51

Summer Berry Limeade. . . .51

Strawberry Shortcake
   Smoothie. 52

Citrus Fruit Cooler 55

Banana Blueberry
   Meal Replacement
   Smoothie. 55

Almond Cake Shake. 57

The Best Darn Green Juice

The secret's out! Green juice is in. I get asked a lot, "Why juice when you can blend?" Such a great question! The answer is that each has different benefits. I'm a big fan of keeping food intact. It was made together for a reason, which means I like blending primarily. Because the whole food stays intact and the fibrous pulp is not removed, a smoothie will keep you feeling fuller longer. It's slower to absorb into the bloodstream, potentially creating lower blood sugar spikes, and it creates no food waste!

Juicing, on the other hand, is a fantastic way to increase your micronutrient load. It gives instant energy because your body doesn't have to break down as much fiber. It decreases the burden on the body because it doesn't have to work as hard on digesting.

So, both blending and juicing are great options, and both have their place. I typically opt for a juice when my autoimmune disease is flaring or I feel very bloated after a night of drinking or consuming inflammatory foods. I want to give my body as much energy as possible to work on healing instead of bogging it down with more work.

This is my go-to green juice recipe. If you don't have a juicer, you can blend this in your blender and strain it through a fine-mesh strainer. I hope you love it as much as I do!

Serves 1 to 2

½ bunch kale

4 fresh parsley stems with leaves

½ English cucumber

1 lime, peeled

4 stalks celery

2 green apples, cored and sliced

Combine all of the ingredients in a juicer, in order, and process. Enjoy immediately or store in the refrigerator for up to 3 days.

Tropical Greens

Spirulina powder is high in vitamins K, A, B1, B2, and B12. It's also a great source of iron, chromium, zinc, magnesium, chlorophyll, phytonutrients, antioxidants, and essential amino acids—the building blocks of protein (GLA, omega-3, -6, and -9). It delivers 7 grams of protein per tablespoon and has more antioxidants than 5 servings of fruits and vegetables. This helps you feel strong and sustained all day long. It typically has a highly identifiable earthy flavor, but that is totally canceled out when you pair it with orange juice. So, enjoy all the benefits of spirulina with this smoothie and none of the drawbacks!

Serves 2

1 cup fresh orange juice

1 cup frozen pineapple chunks

½ cup frozen mango chunks

1 large handful baby spinach

1 to 2 tablespoons spirulina powder

Combine all of the ingredients in a high-powered blender, in order, and blend on high for 30 seconds. Serve immediately.

Sangria Smoothie

This nonalcoholic smoothie is reminiscent of a favorite adult drink, but it's actually good for your microbiome! Add a handful of spinach—you won't even taste it—for a serving of veggies.

Serves 1

1 cup red or green grapes

1 mandarin orange, peeled

⅓ cup fresh or frozen pineapple chunks

¼ medium red apple, cored and sliced

1 tablespoon fresh lemon juice

1 cup ice cubes

Combine all of the ingredients in a high-powered blender, in order, and blend on high for 30 seconds. Serve immediately.

Creamy Peach-Orange Smoothie

This is a great smoothie to bulk up with a scoop of vanilla protein powder or a tablespoon of spirulina. Spirulina can often overpower a smoothie, but I find that orange juice disguises the bitterness and earthy taste quite well. And it's so good for you!

Serves 1

1 cup frozen peach slices

1 medium frozen banana

½ cup fresh orange juice

½ cup unsweetened almond (or other) milk, homemade (page 234) or store-bought

¼ teaspoon pure vanilla extract

Combine all of the ingredients in a high-powered blender, in order, and blend on high for 30 seconds. Serve immediately.

Summer Berry Limeade

This simple and refreshing summer drink contains only three ingredients and is so much better for you than the drive-thru version! Made with real citrus and fruit and sweetened naturally with dates, this is a healthy twist on a summer classic.

Serves 2

1½ cups frozen mixed berries

Juice of 2 limes

3 pitted Medjool dates

1 cup water

Combine all of the ingredients in a high-powered blender, in order, and blend on high for 30 seconds. Serve immediately.

Strawberry Shortcake Smoothie

This smoothie tastes like strawberry shortcake in a cup, only healthier! If you are trying to hit protein goals, you can add a scoop of strawberry or cake-flavored protein powder to intensify the flavor even more! If you do add a sweetened protein powder, omit the maple syrup so it isn't overly sweet.

Serves 2

1¼ cups frozen strawberries

1 large frozen banana

¾ cup canned full-fat coconut milk

2 tablespoons walnuts

1 tablespoon 100% pure maple syrup

1 teaspoon pure vanilla extract

¼ teaspoon ground cinnamon

½ cup ice cubes

Combine all of the ingredients in a high-powered blender, in order, and blend on high for 30 seconds. Serve immediately.

Citrus Fruit Cooler

This juice is delightfully tart and citrusy, with just a hint of sweetness from the orange. The acidity is great for waking up your digestion in the morning. If you don't have a juicer, you can blend this in your blender, then strain it through a fine-mesh strainer.

Serves 2

2 medium oranges, peeled

1 large grapefruit, peeled

1 lemon, peeled

½ lime, peeled

1 large cucumber

Combine all of the ingredients in a juicer, in order, and process. Enjoy immediately or store in the refrigerator for up to 3 days.

Banana Blueberry Meal Replacement Smoothie

Power up with this meal replacement smoothie. Full of healthy fats, complete proteins, fruits, and veggies, this will keep you feeling full and energized. Nutritionally, most protein powders are not sufficient as meal replacements, but with the addition of fiber, fruits, vegetables, whole grains, and fat, this smoothie covers all the bases.

Serves 1

1 cup kale or spinach leaves

1 cup unsweetened vanilla almond (or other) milk, homemade (page 234) or store-bought

1 cup frozen blueberries

1 medium frozen banana

2 tablespoons old-fashioned rolled oats

1 tablespoon almond butter

1 scoop protein powder (optional)

Combine all of the ingredients in a high-powered blender, in order, and blend on high for 30 seconds. Serve immediately.

Almond Cake Shake

Not only is this a show-stopping beauty of a drink, but it tastes like something you'd get at a fancy restaurant. I can't explain exactly why, but when everything comes together, it actually tastes like an Almond Joy– flavored cake, in shake form! With lots of healthy fats from the almonds and coconut, and extra fiber from the dates, this is a great recipe when you want to indulge but still nourish your body with whole foods. If you love coconut and chocolate, this one's for you.

Serves 2

FOR THE CHOCOLATE SAUCE

2 tablespoons cacao powder

2 tablespoons 100% pure maple syrup

2 tablespoons canned full-fat coconut milk

FOR THE SHAKE

¾ cup canned full-fat coconut milk

1 tablespoon 100% pure maple syrup

¼ teaspoon almond extract

2 large pitted Medjool dates

2 tablespoons sliced almonds

2 tablespoons unsweetened shredded coconut

1½ large frozen bananas

1 cup ice cubes

1 In a small bowl, whisk together the cacao powder, maple syrup, and coconut milk until smooth.

2 Combine the coconut milk, maple syrup, almond extract, dates, almonds, 1½ tablespoons of the shredded coconut, the bananas, and ice, in order, in a high-powered blender. Blend on high for 60 seconds, or until smooth.

3 Divide the chocolate sauce evenly between two tall glasses, followed by the shake. Top each glass evenly with the remaining ½ tablespoon coconut.

Morning Quickies

The Best Gluten-Free
Banana Bread. 60

Southern Shrimp and
Cauliflower Grits 62

Old-Fashioned Lemon
Berry Skillet Cake. 64

The Best Pancakes
Ever 66

Dried Fig and Pecan
Oatmeal. 67

Blueberry Chia Seed
Muffins 68

Sweet Potato Frittata 71

Chocolate Peanut Butter
Baked Oats 72

The Best Chia Seed
Pudding. 73

The Best Gluten-Free Banana Bread

Banana bread lovers, look no further! Who says you can't have warm, delicious banana bread just because you've gone gluten-free? Forget about all those premade, gum-filled flour substitutes in the store. This whole grain mixture is just as tasty—and better for you!

Serves 6 to 8

Cooking oil spray

1½ cups old-fashioned rolled oats or oat flour

3 medium, very ripe bananas, peeled and mashed

¼ cup extra-virgin olive oil

¼ cup 100% pure maple syrup

1 large egg

1 teaspoon pure vanilla extract

¾ cup superfine blanched almond flour

1 teaspoon aluminum-free baking powder

½ teaspoon baking soda

¼ teaspoon fine sea salt

¾ cup chopped raw walnuts, chocolate chips, or blueberries (optional)

1   Preheat the oven to 350°F. Spray a 9 × 5-inch loaf pan with cooking oil spray.

2   If using oats, blend them in a high-powered blender on high until they become flour, about 30 seconds. Set aside.

3   In a large bowl or the bowl of a stand mixer, combine the bananas, olive oil, maple syrup, egg, and vanilla.

4   Using a hand mixer or stand mixer, mix on medium-low until well combined.

5   Add the oat flour, almond flour, baking powder, baking soda, and salt. Mix on medium-low until the ingredients are well incorporated and a batter forms. If desired, gently stir in the walnuts, chocolate chips, or blueberries.

6   Pour the batter into the prepared pan. Bake for 25 minutes, then place a piece of aluminum foil over the top to prevent overbrowning. Bake for an additional 20 to 30 minutes, or until a toothpick inserted into the center of the loaf comes out clean.

7   Remove the loaf from the oven and let cool for 15 minutes before serving.

Southern Shrimp and Cauliflower Grits

I lived for a decade in Texas, where shrimp and grits are a breakfast staple. Instead of using traditional grits, which can be a bit carb-heavy, this is a lightened-up version using cauliflower rice instead. If you don't have any cauli-rice on hand, you can grate a large head of cauliflower on a box grater or pulse in a food processor.

Serves 4

FOR THE SHRIMP

6 strips nitrate-free bacon, chopped

1 orange bell pepper, seeded and julienned

½ medium yellow onion, thinly sliced

1 pound large shrimp, peeled and deveined

1½ tablespoons Cajun seasoning, homemade (page 238) or store-bought

1 tablespoon extra-virgin olive oil

¼ cup arrowroot powder

1 Roma tomato, diced

1 cup chicken broth, homemade (page 243) or store-bought

FOR THE GRITS

4 tablespoons salted butter or ghee

4 to 5 cups fresh or frozen cauliflower rice

2 cups chicken broth, homemade (page 243) or store-bought

¼ cup freshly grated Parmesan cheese

1 teaspoon fine sea salt

½ teaspoon ground black pepper

1 Preheat an electric pressure cooker using the **SAUTÉ** function.

2 When the display panel reads **HOT**, add the bacon, bell pepper, and onion and stir until the onion has softened and begins to appear translucent, about 5 minutes.

3 In a large bowl, combine the shrimp, Cajun seasoning, olive oil, and arrowroot powder. Mix well to combine. The mixture will be thick.

4 Add the shrimp mixture, tomato, and broth to the pressure cooker. Stir to combine.

5 Place the lid on the pressure cooker and make sure the vent valve is in the **SEALING** position. Select the **MANUAL/PRESSURE COOK** function and **HIGH PRESSURE**. Use the +/- buttons until the display reads 3 minutes.

6 While the shrimp cooks, make the grits. Preheat a large cast-iron skillet over medium-high heat. Add the butter and cauliflower and sauté for 8 minutes. Add the broth and turn the heat down to medium. Stir occasionally until the liquid is gone and the cauliflower is soft but not mushy, about 10 minutes. Add the cheese, salt, and pepper and keep warm until ready to serve.

7 When the cooker beeps, switch the vent valve from the **SEALING** to the **VENTING** position. Use caution while the steam escapes.

8 Stir the shrimp mixture in the pot. Serve over the cauliflower grits.

Old-Fashioned Lemon Berry Skillet Cake

Pancakes are easy to make, but they can sometimes be a time suck as you stand over the stove making one batch at a time. This skillet cake is like a big, fluffy pancake that you can top with all your favorite traditional pancake toppings. I like to use Pamela's gluten-free pancake mix, but you can use whatever you have on hand.

Serves 8

Cooking oil spray

4 large eggs

2 cups plain Greek yogurt or dairy-free yogurt of choice

¼ cup 100% pure maple syrup, plus more for drizzling

Grated zest of 1 lemon, plus 2 tablespoons lemon juice

1 teaspoon pure vanilla extract

1 teaspoon almond extract

1½ cups pancake mix

1 tablespoon aluminum-free baking powder

1 cup fresh or frozen mixed berries, plus more fresh berries for topping (optional)

Powdered sugar, for sprinkling (optional)

1 Preheat the oven to 350°F. Spray a large cast-iron skillet with cooking oil spray.

2 In a large bowl or the bowl of a stand mixer, combine the eggs, yogurt, maple syrup, lemon zest, lemon juice, vanilla extract, and almond extract.

3 Using a hand mixer or stand mixer, mix on low until combined.

4 Add the pancake mix and baking powder. Mix on medium-low until the ingredients are well incorporated and a batter forms. Gently stir in the berries.

5 Pour the batter into the prepared skillet. Bake for 35 to 40 minutes, or until a toothpick inserted into the center of the cake comes out clean.

6 Remove the cake from the oven and let cool for 10 minutes. Serve with a drizzle of maple syrup, a sprinkle of powdered sugar (if desired), and some fresh berries (if desired).

The Best Pancakes Ever

Who doesn't love pancakes for dinner? These fluffy, gluten-free pancakes taste just like the gluten-full ones we grew up on. The almond flour makes them super soft, but the cassava ensures that they have that perfect golden crisp on the outside edge that makes a pancake so very good.

If you prefer not to use a blender, you can simply whisk the eggs until frothy in a large bowl, and combine the wet ingredients before adding the dry. Just make sure you use oat flour instead of old-fashioned oats.

Makes 18 to 20 pancakes

6 large eggs

¾ cup unsweetened almond (or other) milk, homemade (page 234) or store-bought

2 tablespoons raw honey

2 teaspoons pure vanilla extract

1 cup tightly packed superfine blanched almond flour

½ cup old-fashioned rolled oats or oat flour

½ cup cassava flour

2 teaspoons baking soda

1 teaspoon fine sea salt

Cooking oil spray or butter

½ cup mini chocolate chips

Peanut butter, optional

100% pure maple syrup, and/or ground cinnamon, for topping (optional)

1 Preheat a large cast-iron skillet or electric griddle over medium-low heat.

2 Put the eggs in a high-powered blender and blend on high until frothy, about 15 seconds. Add the milk, honey, vanilla extract, almond flour, oats, cassava flour, baking soda, and salt. Blend on high until the mixture forms a batter, about 1 minute.

3 Use cooking oil spray or butter to grease your skillet or griddle. Using a ¼-cup measuring cup, spoon the batter onto your preheated surface. Smooth it out with the back of the cup to make a perfect circle. Sprinkle each pancake with chocolate chips.

4 Cook the pancakes for 3 minutes on each side, or until cooked through and lightly browned. Almond flour gets dark much more quickly than regular flour, so watch closely and adjust the heat accordingly.

5 Serve topped with peanut butter, maple syrup, and a pinch of cinnamon, if desired.

Dried Fig and Pecan Oatmeal

We love a good bowl of oatmeal in our house. We make an oat-based breakfast at least twice a week. Three years ago, we planted an orchard with two fig trees, and now we have an abundance of figs at the end of every summer. This is one of our favorite ways to incorporate them into our meals. If you can't find fresh figs, Costco carries a bag of dried organic figs and those will work just the same! You can also use old-fashioned rolled oats if you do not have steel-cut.

Serves 4

3 cups water

1 cup steel-cut oats

8 dried or fresh figs, diced

2 tablespoons 100% pure maple syrup

1 tablespoon ground cinnamon

½ teaspoon fine sea salt

¼ cup chopped raw pecans

1 In an electric pressure cooker, combine the water, oats, figs, maple syrup, cinnamon, and salt.

2 Place the lid on the pressure cooker and make sure the vent valve is in the **SEALING** position. Select the **MANUAL/PRESSURE COOK** function and **HIGH PRESSURE**. Use the +/- buttons until the display reads 12 minutes.

3 When the cooker beeps, switch the vent valve from the **SEALING** to the **VENTING** position. Use caution while the steam escapes.

4 Top the oatmeal with the pecans and serve immediately.

Blueberry Chia Seed Muffins

Grain-, dairy-, and sugar-free, these little bits of heaven are bound to become a fast favorite! They disappear quickly whenever I make a batch. Unfortunately, you cannot sub in any other flour for the coconut flour. Coconut flour is unlike anything else and is incredibly absorbent, so expect the batter to be very thick.

Makes 18 muffins

1 cup coconut flour

1 teaspoon baking soda

½ teaspoon fine sea salt

6 large eggs

½ cup canned full-fat coconut milk

½ cup plus 2 tablespoons raw honey

¼ cup grated lemon zest

½ cup fresh lemon juice

¼ cup extra-virgin olive oil

4 teaspoons pure vanilla extract

¼ cup chia seeds

1 cup fresh blueberries

1 Preheat the oven to 350°F. Line a standard 12-cup muffin pan with paper or silicone liners.

2 Sift the coconut flour, baking soda, and salt into a small bowl.

3 In a large bowl, whisk together the eggs, coconut milk, honey, lemon zest, lemon juice, olive oil, and vanilla. Add the chia seeds and whisk until combined. Let the mixture sit for 10 minutes.

4 Pour the flour mixture into the wet ingredients and mix well. Fold ½ cup of the blueberries into the mixture.

5 Fill the lined muffin cups three-quarters full. Sprinkle each with some of the remaining blueberries.

6 Bake for 25 to 30 minutes, or until the muffins are golden and a toothpick inserted in the center comes out clean. Remove the muffins with their liners from the pan and let cool on a rack.

7 Place new liners in 6 of the muffin cups and repeat with the remaining batter to make the rest of the muffins.

Sweet Potato Frittata

This is one of my favorite breakfasts of all time. I've been making this recipe for about a decade, and it's one that everyone loves. Add more veggies if you have some that need to be used or keep it super simple as is. Serve it solo or with your favorite ketchup, salsa, or sriracha.

Serves 6

1 tablespoon extra-virgin olive oil

3 shallots, sliced thinly

1 large sweet potato, diced

2 tablespoons water

1 large handful baby spinach

10 large eggs

1 teaspoon fine sea salt

½ teaspoon ground black pepper

½ teaspoon garlic powder

6 strips nitrate-free bacon, cooked and crumbled

1 Preheat the oven to 375°F.

2 Heat a large cast-iron skillet over medium-high heat. Add the olive oil, shallots, and sweet potato and cook, stirring occasionally, until the potato begins to soften, about 10 minutes. Add the water and allow the potato to cook down until fully tender, about 4 more minutes.

3 Add the spinach and toss just until wilted.

4 In a large bowl, whisk together the eggs, salt, pepper, and garlic powder.

5 Pour the eggs into the skillet, but do *not* stir. Let cook until the edges of the eggs have started to set, about 2 minutes. Turn off the heat and sprinkle the top with the bacon.

6 Transfer the skillet to the oven and bake for 20 to 30 minutes, or until the eggs have set.

7 Slice and serve warm.

Chocolate Peanut Butter Baked Oats

My kids call this chocolate breakfast cake! It is so easy and tasty and is a fantastic breakfast for meal-prep, as it'll keep in the refrigerator for a week. If you're not making your own plant milk, I like the MALK brand as it has the fewest ingredients. Their chocolate almond milk is absolutely spectacular with a drizzle of maple syrup. Kiki Milk is another great option.

Serves 12

Cooking oil spray

3 large eggs

1¾ cups unsweetened chocolate or vanilla almond (or other) milk, homemade (page 234) or store-bought

½ cup 100% pure maple syrup

½ cup peanut butter

1 teaspoon pure vanilla extract

3 cups old-fashioned rolled oats

2 tablespoons ground flax seed

1 teaspoon aluminum-free baking powder

½ cup chocolate chips

1 Preheat the oven to 350°F. Spray a 9 × 13-inch glass baking dish with cooking oil spray.

2 In a large bowl or the bowl of a stand mixer, combine the eggs, milk, maple syrup, peanut butter, and vanilla.

3 Using a hand mixer or stand mixer, mix on low until combined.

4 Add the oats, flax seed, and baking powder. Mix on medium-low until the ingredients are well incorporated and a batter forms.

5 Pour the batter into the prepared baking dish and sprinkle with the chocolate chips. Bake for 40 minutes.

6 Remove from the oven and let cool for 10 minutes before serving.

The Best Chia Seed Pudding

Chia pudding keeps well in the refrigerator for up to 5 days, but I promise this will be long gone before then. Sweet and scrumptious, this is the perfect fibrous after-dinner delight. Sometimes I even eat it for breakfast! I like to use applesauce because it's easy and I always have it on hand, but this recipe also works fabulously with other fruit purees, like mashed mangoes, raspberries, strawberries, or plums.

Serves 2 to 4

1 cup applesauce or other fruit puree

1 cup canned full-fat coconut milk

¼ cup chia seeds

2 teaspoons 100% pure maple syrup

Combine all of the ingredients in a mason jar and mix well with a spoon. Cover and refrigerate for at least 1 hour before serving. Serve chilled.

Super Soups

Greek Lemon-Dill
   Chicken Soup 77

Creamy Beet Bisque. 78

Salmon Chowder 79

Ginger-Turmeric
   Chicken Stew 80

Pumpkin Bisque 82

Jalapeño Popper
   Chicken Chili 84

Caribbean Mango and
   Black Bean Stew 86

Chicken Pot Pie Soup. 87

Italian Wedding Soup 89

Greek Lemon-Dill Chicken Soup

This deliciously dill-filled and comforting chicken soup is the perfect spring/summertime soup. Made with fresh herbs and summer vegetables, it doesn't feel heavy and is light and refreshing. If you are eating plant-based, you can replace the chicken with 2 cans of chickpeas, rinsed and drained.

Serves 6

1 tablespoon extra-virgin olive oil

1 pound boneless, skinless chicken breasts

1 cup wild rice

½ yellow onion, diced

3 large carrots, diced

3 celery stalks, diced

6 cloves garlic, minced

6 cups chicken or vegetable broth, homemade (page 243 or 244) or store-bought

Juice of 2 lemons, plus lemon wedges for serving

2 teaspoons fine sea salt, plus more to taste

1½ teaspoons ground black pepper, plus more to taste

1 teaspoon dried oregano

1 large zucchini, diced

1 tablespoon chopped fresh dill, plus more for serving (optional)

1 tablespoon chopped fresh parsley, plus more for serving (optional)

1 In an electric pressure cooker, combine the olive oil, chicken, wild rice, onion, carrots, celery, garlic, broth, lemon juice, salt, pepper, and oregano and stir.

2 Place the lid on the cooker and make sure the vent valve is in the **SEALING** position. Select the **MANUAL/PRESSURE COOK** function and **HIGH PRESSURE**. Use the +/- buttons until the display reads 22 minutes.

3 When the cooker beeps, let it naturally release the pressure until the display reads **LO:05**. Switch the vent valve from the **SEALING** to the **VENTING** position. Use caution while the steam escapes.

4 Shred the chicken into the juices with two forks. Stir in the zucchini, dill, and parsley. Place the lid back on the cooker and allow the zucchini to cook in the residual heat until tender, about 5 minutes.

5 Season with salt and pepper as needed and serve warm with lemon wedges and additional fresh herbs, if desired.

Creamy Beet Bisque

This delightful bisque is a great way to get the earthy-tasting vegetable into your diet in a delicious way! I promise this is a winning dish even if you don't love the taste of beets. In a blind taste test, my husband said it tasted like a cheesy cheddar soup. I've worked hard to make this bisque ultra-palatable for even your pickiest eater!

Serves 2 to 4

1 tablespoon extra-virgin olive oil

½ red onion, diced

2 beets, cubed

2 cloves garlic, minced

1 tablespoon chopped fresh ginger

¼ cup chopped fresh parsley

¼ cup chopped fresh cilantro stems, plus cilantro leaves for serving (optional)

½ cup stemmed kale

½ cup raw cashews

1 (13.5-ounce) can full-fat coconut milk

1 cup vegetable broth, homemade (page 244) or store-bought

1 teaspoon fine sea salt, plus more to taste

Ground black pepper, to taste

2 tablespoons fresh lemon juice

1 Preheat an electric pressure cooker using the **SAUTÉ** function.

2 When the display panel reads **HOT**, add the olive oil, onion, and beets and stir until the onion has softened and begins to appear translucent.

3 Add the garlic and stir until fragrant, about 1 minute.

4 Add the ginger, parsley, cilantro stems, kale, cashews, coconut milk, broth, salt, pepper, and lemon juice.

5 Place the lid on the pressure cooker and make sure the vent valve is in the **SEALING** position. Select the **MANUAL/PRESSURE COOK** function and **HIGH PRESSURE**. Use the +/- buttons until the display reads 10 minutes.

6 When the cooker beeps, switch the vent valve from the **SEALING** to the **VENTING** position. Use caution while the steam escapes.

7 Remove the lid of the pressure cooker and puree the soup using an immersion blender.

8 Let cool for 10 minutes, then season with salt and pepper as needed and serve with a sprinkle of cilantro leaves, if desired.

Salmon Chowder

Made with fresh salmon, creamy potatoes, and a rich broth, this hearty chowder makes a filling weeknight dinner. I prefer wild-caught salmon because it's more nutritionally dense than farm-raised and can contain one-third as much fat, fewer calories, and more vitamins and minerals.

Serves 6

1 tablespoon salted butter, ghee, or extra-virgin olive oil

1 large yellow onion, finely chopped

4 stalks celery, finely chopped

1 pound red potatoes, cut into 1-inch cubes

4 cloves garlic, minced

4 cups chicken broth, homemade (page 243) or store-bought

1 (13.5-ounce) can full-fat coconut milk

½ teaspoon dried thyme

1½ teaspoons fine sea salt

½ teaspoon ground black pepper

1½ pounds wild-caught Alaskan salmon, skin and pin bones removed, cut into ½-inch pieces

¼ cup arrowroot powder

¼ cup cold water

¼ cup chopped fresh chives (optional)

1 Preheat an electric pressure cooker using the **SAUTÉ** function.

2 When the display panel reads **HOT**, add the butter, onion, celery, and potatoes. Cook, stirring occasionally, until the onion is translucent, about 5 minutes. Stir in the minced garlic and cook for 1 minute.

3 Add the broth, coconut milk, thyme, salt, pepper, and salmon and stir to combine.

4 Place the lid on the cooker and make sure the vent valve is in the **SEALING** position. Select the **MANUAL/ PRESSURE COOK** function and **HIGH PRESSURE**. Use the +/- buttons until the display reads 10 minutes.

5 When the cooker beeps, let it naturally release the pressure until the display reads **LO:05**. Switch the vent valve from the **SEALING** to the **VENTING** position. Use caution while the steam escapes.

6 In a small bowl, whisk together the arrowroot powder and water. Stir into the chowder until the sauce thickens.

7 Garnish with the chives, if desired, and serve.

Ginger-Turmeric Chicken Stew

This rustic stew is a powerhouse filled with ginger, garlic, and turmeric, ingredients that are proven to support our immune system. You can boost its health properties even more by stirring in a little miso or spinach at the end.

Garlic is a plant in the allium (onion) family. Scientists have found that most of garlic's health benefits are caused by sulfur compounds (allicin) formed when the clove is chopped, crushed, or chewed. These compounds have been shown to boost the disease-fighting response of some types of white blood cells in the body.

Ginger is a strong antioxidant that can naturally boost the immune system. It can help kill cold viruses and is packed with beneficial vitamins like magnesium, iron, zinc, and calcium.

Turmeric helps bolster the immune system by increasing the immunomodulating capacity of the body. It's a dark yellow warm spice that comes from the root of the curcuma plant. Curcumin, a compound found in turmeric, is known to have anti-inflammatory properties that help boost immunity.

This comforting stew tastes so good, its healing powers are almost secondary.

Serves 4 to 6

1 large yellow onion, diced

1 head celery, roughly chopped

3 large carrots, roughly chopped

1½ pounds baby creamer potatoes, cut in half

1 medium sweet potato, roughly chopped

1 pound boneless, skinless chicken breasts, cut into ½-inch cubes

6 cloves garlic, minced

2 tablespoons coconut aminos or low-sodium soy sauce

1 tablespoon grated fresh ginger

2 teaspoons ground turmeric

1 Preheat an electric pressure cooker using the **SAUTÉ** function.

2 When the display panel reads **HOT**, add the onion, celery, and carrots to the pot. Stir every couple of minutes until the vegetables soften and the onion begins to become translucent, about 5 minutes. (This is called a dry sauté, using the vegetables' natural water content to cook them down.)

3 Add the potatoes, chicken, and garlic. Stir and let the garlic become fragrant, about 1 minute.

4 Add the coconut aminos, ginger, turmeric, dried parsley, onion powder, garlic powder, salt, black pepper, and red pepper flakes and stir to combine. Then add the broth.

5 Place the lid on the pressure cooker and make sure the vent valve is in the **SEALING** position. Select the

1 tablespoon dried parsley

1 tablespoon onion powder

1 tablespoon garlic powder

1 teaspoon fine sea salt

½ teaspoon ground black pepper

¼ teaspoon red pepper flakes

2 cups chicken broth, homemade (page 243) or store-bought

2 tablespoons chopped fresh parsley or chives (optional)

MANUAL/**PRESSURE COOK** function and **HIGH PRESSURE**. Use the +/- buttons until the display reads 6 minutes.

6 When the cooker beeps, let it naturally release the pressure until the display reads **LO:05**. Switch the vent valve from the **SEALING** to the **VENTING** position. Use caution while the steam escapes.

7 Let cool for 5 minutes, then serve topped with fresh parsley or chives, if desired.

Pumpkin Bisque

Don't let the fact that this soup is pumpkin-based limit it to fall—it's a fantastic soup to consume all year round. The vegetables are the star of the show, and the light, classic fall spices add a hint of cozy nostalgia. Depending on the broth you use, you might need to adjust the salt and pepper. Homemade broths tend to have lower sodium levels. As always, make sure to taste before you serve so you can adjust to your liking.

Serves 6

2 tablespoons salted butter, ghee, or extra-virgin olive oil

1 medium yellow onion, diced

2 medium carrots, diced

1 medium sweet potato, diced

2 cloves garlic, minced

1 teaspoon ground cinnamon

¼ teaspoon ground ginger

⅛ teaspoon ground nutmeg

1½ teaspoons fine sea salt

½ teaspoon ground black pepper

3½ cups vegetable or chicken broth, homemade (page 244 or 243), or store-bought

2 (14-ounce) cans pumpkin puree

1 (13.5-ounce) can full-fat coconut milk

2 tablespoons 100% pure maple syrup

2 tablespoons roasted pumpkin seeds (optional)

2 tablespoons pomegranate seeds (optional)

2 tablespoons Greek yogurt (optional)

1 Preheat an electric pressure cooker using the **SAUTÉ** function.

2 When the display panel reads **HOT**, add the butter, onion, carrots, and sweet potato. Cook, stirring occasionally, until the onion is translucent, about 5 minutes.

3 Stir in the garlic, cinnamon, ginger, nutmeg, salt, and pepper and cook for 1 minute.

4 Add the broth, pumpkin puree, coconut milk, and maple syrup and stir to combine.

5 Place the lid on the cooker and make sure the vent valve is in the **SEALING** position. Select the **MANUAL/PRESSURE COOK** function and **HIGH PRESSURE**. Use the +/- buttons until the display reads 12 minutes.

6 When the cooker beeps, let it naturally release the pressure until the display reads **LO:05**. Switch the vent valve from the **SEALING** to the **VENTING** position. Use caution while the steam escapes.

7 Remove the lid of the pressure cooker and puree the soup using an immersion blender.

8 Serve garnished with the roasted pumpkin seeds, pomegranate seeds, and a swirl of yogurt, if desired.

Jalapeño Popper Chicken Chili

Full of flavor, this chicken chili has a little kick of heat, but not so much that you'll need to keep a glass of water nearby. I love it as is, but my kids like to top it with a little sour cream, shredded cheese, a sprinkle of finely diced jalapeño, and tortilla chips. It will last in the fridge for up to 6 days and keeps getting better the longer it sits. This is a great soup to prep for lunches for the week!

Serves 6

1 tablespoon extra-virgin olive oil

6 strips nitrate-free bacon, chopped

3 jalapeños, seeded and finely chopped

1 medium yellow onion, finely chopped

1 large red bell pepper, seeded and finely chopped

4 cloves garlic, minced

1½ pounds boneless, skinless chicken breasts, cut into 1-inch pieces

1 (15-ounce) can pinto beans, rinsed and drained

1 (14.5-ounce) can diced tomatoes with juices

1 (15-ounce) can tomato sauce

½ cup frozen corn

1 cup chicken broth, homemade (page 243) or store-bought

1 tablespoon chili powder

2 teaspoons fine sea salt

1 teaspoon ground black pepper

½ teaspoon red pepper flakes

⅓ cup ranch dressing, homemade (page 153) or store-bought

1 Preheat an electric pressure cooker using the **SAUTÉ** function.

2 When the display panel reads **HOT**, add the olive oil, bacon, jalapeños, onion, and bell pepper. Cook, stirring occasionally, until the onion is translucent and the bacon begins to crisp, about 10 minutes. Stir in the minced garlic and cook for 1 minute.

3 Add the chicken, pinto beans, tomatoes, tomato sauce, corn, broth, chili powder, salt, black pepper, and red pepper flakes and stir to combine.

4 Place the lid on the cooker and make sure the vent valve is in the **SEALING** position. Select the **MANUAL/ PRESSURE COOK** function and **HIGH PRESSURE**. Use the +/- buttons until the display reads 16 minutes.

5 When the cooker beeps, let it naturally release the pressure until the display reads **LO:05**. Switch the vent valve from the **SEALING** to the **VENTING** position. Use caution while the steam escapes.

6 Stir in the ranch dressing. Serve warm.

Caribbean Mango and Black Bean Stew

This Caribbean-inspired stew is hearty and delicious. If you do not eat pork, you can substitute chicken or leave it out entirely and add lentils as a vegan protein source.

Serves 4

1 pound pork tenderloin, cut into 1-inch pieces

1 teaspoon fine sea salt

½ teaspoon ground black pepper

1 tablespoon coconut oil

2 medium sweet potatoes, cut into 1-inch cubes

1 medium yellow onion, diced

4 cloves garlic, minced

1 cup diced mango

1 (15-ounce) can black beans, rinsed and drained

1 (14.5-ounce) can diced tomatoes with juices

1 cup tomato sauce

½ cup water

1 tablespoon sriracha

1 teaspoon dried thyme

1 teaspoon dried oregano

1   In a medium bowl, toss the pork with the salt and pepper.

2   Preheat an electric pressure cooker using the **SAUTÉ** function.

3   When the display panel reads **HOT**, add the coconut oil and pork. Cook, stirring occasionally, until the pork is browned, about 4 minutes.

4   Add the sweet potatoes, onion, garlic, mango, black beans, tomatoes, tomato sauce, water, sriracha, thyme, and oregano and stir to combine.

5   Place the lid on the cooker and make sure the vent valve is in the **SEALING** position. Select the **MANUAL/PRESSURE COOK** function and **HIGH PRESSURE**. Use the +/- buttons until the display reads 15 minutes.

6   When the cooker beeps, let it naturally release the pressure until the display reads **LO:05**. Switch the vent valve from the **SEALING** to the **VENTING** position. Use caution while the steam escapes.

7   Ladle the stew into bowls and serve.

Chicken Pot Pie Soup

My mom used to buy the big boxes of individual Marie Callender's pot pies when I was growing up, and I don't know if there was anything better than one of those things fresh out of the oven. The buttery, flaky crust, the deliciously creamy vegetables, and the cream-stuffed center. I tried to re-create the feel of this weeknight dinner classic in soup form, and I think I did a pretty bang-up job! This version isn't as calorically dense, is dairy-free, and still maintains the flavor of the pie we all loved so much!

Serves 4 to 6

FOR THE SOUP

1 tablespoon ghee or extra-virgin olive oil

1 medium yellow onion, diced

4 medium carrots, diced

4 stalks celery, diced

6 cloves garlic, minced

1½ pounds boneless, skinless chicken breasts, cut into ½-inch pieces

1 large russet potato, cut into 1-inch cubes

½ cup frozen green beans

½ cup frozen peas

4 cups chicken broth, homemade (page 243) or store-bought

1½ teaspoons dried sage

1 teaspoon dried rosemary

½ teaspoon ground nutmeg

2 teaspoons fine sea salt

¾ teaspoon ground black pepper

¼ cup chopped fresh parsley (optional)

FOR THE CASHEW CREAM

1 cup raw cashews, soaked for 4 hours and drained

½ to ⅔ cup water

1 Preheat an electric pressure cooker using the **SAUTÉ** function.

2 When the display panel reads **HOT**, add the ghee, onion, carrots, and celery. Cook, stirring occasionally, until the onion is translucent, about 5 minutes. Stir in the garlic and cook for 1 minute.

3 Add the chicken, potato, green beans, peas, broth, sage, rosemary, nutmeg, salt, and pepper and stir to combine.

4 Place the lid on the cooker and make sure the vent valve is in the **SEALING** position. Select the **MANUAL/PRESSURE COOK** function and **HIGH PRESSURE**. Use the +/- buttons until the display reads 16 minutes.

5 Meanwhile, make the cashew cream: In a blender, blend the cashews and water for 1 minute or until thick and creamy. Add more water as needed. Set aside.

6 When the cooker beeps, let it naturally release the pressure until the display reads **LO:05**. Switch the vent valve from the **SEALING** to the **VENTING** position. Use caution while the steam escapes.

7 Stir in the cashew cream and serve, topped with fresh parsley, if desired.

Italian Wedding Soup

Are you ready for the *best* Italian wedding soup? This is a delicious and hearty soup made with herby bite-size beef meatballs, ditalini, and, of course, Parmesan cheese! Top with salt and freshly ground pepper and any fresh parsley you might have in your garden or refrigerator. I love to serve it with crusty Italian bread spread with grass-fed butter.

Serves 6

FOR THE MEATBALLS

8 ounces grass-fed ground beef

1 large egg

2 tablespoons almond flour

1 tablespoon Italian seasoning, homemade (page 238) or store-bought

½ teaspoon fine sea salt

¼ teaspoon ground black pepper

FOR THE SOUP

2 tablespoons extra-virgin olive oil

1 medium yellow onion, finely chopped

3 medium carrots, diced small

2 stalks celery, diced small

4 cloves garlic, minced

6 cups chicken broth, homemade (page 243) or store-bought

¼ teaspoon dried dill

2 tablespoons chopped fresh parsley

2 cups packed fresh baby spinach

¾ cup gluten-free ditalini or other small pasta

1 cup freshly grated Parmesan cheese (optional)

1   In a medium bowl, combine the ground beef, egg, almond flour, Italian seasoning, salt, and pepper. Using your hands, shape into about 40 tiny balls and place on a plate. Set aside.

2   Preheat an electric pressure cooker using the **SAUTÉ** function.

3   When the display panel reads **HOT**, add the olive oil, onion, carrots, celery, and garlic. Cook, stirring occasionally, until the onion is translucent, about 5 minutes.

4   Add the broth, dill, parsley, spinach, and ditalini and stir to combine. Top with the meatballs in a single layer.

5   Place the lid on the cooker and make sure the vent valve is in the **SEALING** position. Select the **MANUAL/PRESSURE COOK** function and **HIGH PRESSURE**. Use the +/- buttons until the display reads 5 minutes.

6   When the cooker beeps, let it naturally release the pressure until the display reads **LO:10**. Switch the vent valve from the **SEALING** to the **VENTING** position. Use caution while the steam escapes.

7   Ladle into soup bowls and top with Parmesan cheese, if desired.

Snappy Salads

Citrus Chicken Salad 92

Mediterranean Herb
  and Bean Salad 94

Herby Mango Chicken
  Salad 95

Summertime Veggie
  Salad with Lemon
  Tahini Dressing 96

Blueberry Kale Spring
  Green Salad 98

Cobb Salad with Chicken
  Strips and Honey
  Mustard 101

Classic Caesar Salad 103

Chinese-Style
  Cucumber Salad 104

Thai Peanut Chicken
  Salad 105

Citrus Chicken Salad

This salad is so vibrant and full of color—it just makes you feel good to see the bright pops of orange contrasted with the green. The flavor is bright and tangy, with hints of sweet and savory. You can use spring mix, arugula, spinach, or romaine lettuce. If you do not have chives on hand, try subbing in green onions.

Serves 4

FOR THE DRESSING

½ cup extra-virgin olive oil

3 tablespoons white vinegar

1 tablespoon grated
  orange zest

½ cup fresh orange juice

1 tablespoon raw honey

1 tablespoon Dijon mustard

1 teaspoon fine sea salt

½ teaspoon ground black pepper

FOR THE CHICKEN

1 pound boneless, skinless
  chicken breasts

1 teaspoon fine sea salt, plus
  more to taste

½ teaspoon ground black
  pepper, plus more to taste

FOR THE SALAD

5 ounces spring mix

1 large avocado, pitted, peeled,
  and diced

4 ounces crumbled feta
  (optional)

1 orange, peeled and
  segmented

½ cup slivered almonds

¼ cup chopped fresh chives

1 To make the dressing, in a small, wide-mouth jar, combine all of the dressing ingredients and blend using an immersion blender until smooth.

2 Pour half of the dressing into an electric pressure cooker. Add the chicken, salt, and pepper.

3 Place the lid on the pressure cooker and make sure the vent valve is in the **SEALING** position. Select the **MANUAL/PRESSURE COOK** function and **HIGH PRESSURE**. Use the +/- buttons until the display reads 16 minutes.

4 Meanwhile, in a large bowl, combine the spring mix, avocado, feta (if using), orange, almonds, and chives and toss well.

5 When the cooker beeps, let it naturally release the pressure until the display reads **LO:05**. Switch the vent valve from the **SEALING** to the **VENTING** position. Use caution while the steam escapes.

6 Shred the chicken into the juices using two forks.

7 Top the salad with the chicken and drizzle with the remaining dressing. Toss to combine and season with salt and pepper to taste.

Mediterranean Herb and Bean Salad

I like to make this simple, hearty lunch ahead of time because the longer it sits in the fridge, the bolder the flavors become as the beans really take on the flavor of the dressing. This is a great salad to meal-prep as a main or a side.

Serves 2 to 4

2 (15-ounce) cans pinto, navy, and/or black beans, rinsed and drained

1 cup diced cherry tomatoes

½ English cucumber, finely chopped

⅓ cup chopped pitted kalamata olives

¼ cup finely chopped fresh chives

3 tablespoons white wine vinegar

1 tablespoon extra-virgin olive oil

1 tablespoon Dijon mustard

1 teaspoon raw honey

1 teaspoon fine sea salt, plus more to taste

¾ teaspoon ground black pepper, plus more to taste

¼ teaspoon dried oregano

1 In a large bowl, combine all of the ingredients. Toss to coat, then season with additional salt and pepper if needed.

2 Allow the salad to marinate for 15 minutes at room temperature before serving.

Herby Mango Chicken Salad

This is a great make-ahead meal to eat on the go or to take to work for lunch. It is delightful over toasted sourdough with fresh lettuce, as a cracker dip, or made into lettuce cups. It will keep well in an airtight container in the fridge for up to 5 days.

Serves 4 to 6

FOR THE CHICKEN

1 pound boneless, skinless chicken breasts

½ cup chicken broth, homemade (page 243) or store-bought

½ bunch fresh cilantro, stems finely chopped, leaves reserved for salad

1 teaspoon fine sea salt

½ teaspoon ground black pepper

FOR THE SALAD

1½ cups fresh or thawed frozen mango chunks

½ cup mayonnaise, homemade (page 240) or store-bought

2 stalks celery, diced

¼ cup raw cashews, chopped

2 tablespoons finely chopped fresh chives

2 tablespoons fresh cilantro leaves

1   In an electric pressure cooker, combine the chicken, broth, cilantro stems, salt, and pepper.

2   Place the lid on the pressure cooker and make sure the vent valve is in the **SEALING** position. Select the **MANUAL/PRESSURE COOK** function and **HIGH PRESSURE**. Use the **+/-** buttons until the display reads 16 minutes.

3   Meanwhile, in a medium bowl, combine all of the salad ingredients and toss well.

4   When the cooker beeps, let it naturally release the pressure until the display reads **LO:05**. Switch the vent valve from the **SEALING** to the **VENTING** position. Use caution while the steam escapes.

5   Shred the chicken into the juices using two forks.

6   Add the chicken to the salad and toss to combine.

Summertime Veggie Salad with Lemon Tahini Dressing

There is a shortcut to this recipe if you don't cook your legumes from scratch: simply replace the cooked dry lentils with a 15-ounce can of lentils, rinsed and drained, at the end. But honestly, making them in the pressure cooker is better not only for your digestive tract but for your pocketbook, and by the time the vegetables are done roasting, your lentils will be ready too! Or, if you prefer, feel free to replace the lentils with a cooked protein of your choice. This salad pairs really nicely with chicken or salmon.

Serves 4

FOR THE SALAD

¾ cup brown lentils

1 cup vegetable broth, homemade (page 244) or store-bought, or water

2 cups diced sweet potatoes

2 cups diced carrots

1 teaspoon fine sea salt

½ teaspoon ground black pepper

½ teaspoon chili powder

1 tablespoon extra-virgin olive oil

1 medium zucchini, diced

1 medium yellow squash, diced

FOR THE LEMON TAHINI DRESSING

2 tablespoons fresh lemon juice

2 tablespoons Dijon mustard

2 tablespoons tahini, homemade (page 239) or store-bought

¼ cup chopped fresh parsley (optional)

1   In an electric pressure cooker, combine the brown lentils and broth.

2   Place the lid on the cooker and make sure the vent valve is in the **SEALING** position. Select the **MANUAL/PRESSURE COOK** function and **HIGH PRESSURE**. Use the +/- buttons until the display reads 8 minutes.

3   In the basket of a 5.3-quart air fryer, combine the sweet potatoes, carrots, ½ teaspoon of the salt, ¼ teaspoon of the pepper, ¼ teaspoon of the chili powder, and ½ tablespoon of the olive oil. Air-fry for 10 minutes at 390°F.

4   Add the zucchini and squash and the remaining salt, pepper, chili powder, and oil and air-fry for an additional 15 minutes.

5   Meanwhile, in a small bowl, whisk together all of the dressing ingredients except for the parsley.

6   When the cooker beeps, switch the vent valve from the **SEALING** to the **VENTING** position. Use caution while the steam escapes.

7   In a large bowl, combine the lentils, roasted vegetables, and dressing. Sprinkle with the parsley, if desired, and serve warm.

Blueberry Kale Spring Green Salad

Don't waste time shaving each Brussels sprout by hand! Simply trim the ends, cut them in half, and toss them in your high-powered blender. Blend at a variable 2 or 3 speed and you'll have perfectly shaved Brussels sprouts with none of the extra work! This is a giant salad, so make sure your bowl is big enough. Even if you're serving it for a smaller crowd, make the whole thing because it keeps great in the refrigerator for lunches throughout the week.

Serves 6 to 8

FOR THE SALAD

10 ounces shaved Brussels sprouts

2 cups chopped kale

2 cups chopped spinach

2 cups fresh blueberries

1 cup chopped walnuts

1 large avocado, pitted, peeled, and diced

FOR THE DRESSING

⅓ cup extra-virgin olive oil

1 teaspoon grated lemon zest

¼ cup fresh lemon juice

2 tablespoons raw honey

1½ teaspoons Dijon mustard

2 teaspoons garlic powder

½ teaspoon fine sea salt

¼ teaspoon ground black pepper

1 In a large bowl, combine the Brussels sprouts, kale, spinach, blueberries, walnuts, and avocado.

2 In a small, wide-mouth jar, combine all of the dressing ingredients and blend using an immersion blender until smooth.

3 Drizzle the dressing over the salad and toss to combine.

Cobb Salad with Chicken Strips and Honey Mustard

This was my go-to salad for the entire summer of 2023. I could not get enough of it! My friends on Instagram will remember this salad obsession. If you do not have time to make the simple gluten-free chicken strips, I recommend substituting a 1-pound package of Applegate gluten-free chicken tenders or Butcher Box gluten-free chicken nuggets.

Serves 4

FOR THE SALAD

4 cups mixed greens

4 hard-boiled eggs (see page 22), peeled and cut in half

4 strips nitrate-free bacon, cooked and crumbled

2 small to medium avocados, pitted, peeled, and sliced

1 recipe Gluten-Free Chicken Strips (page 177) or store-bought

½ cup pumpkin seeds

FOR THE DRESSING

½ cup mayonnaise, homemade (page 240) or store-bought

2 tablespoons apple cider vinegar

2 tablespoons raw honey

2 tablespoons yellow mustard

1 teaspoon onion powder

¼ teaspoon fine sea salt

1 On a large platter, layer the mixed greens, hard-boiled eggs, bacon, avocados, chicken strips, and pumpkin seeds.

2 In a small, wide-mouth mason jar, combine all of the dressing ingredients and blend using an immersion blender until smooth.

3 Drizzle the salad with the dressing and serve family-style.

Classic Caesar Salad

Hands down, this is the salad I get the most recipe requests for. There isn't a single person who comes to my house and doesn't hail this the best salad they've ever had. I like to use Red Boat fish sauce because it's Whole30 approved and doesn't have any added sugars. My favorite Parmesan cheese is Kirkland Signature Parmigiano-Reggiano; it comes from Italy and you can taste the difference!

Serves 6

FOR THE DRESSING

1 cup mayonnaise, homemade (page 240) or store-bought

½ cup freshly grated Parmesan cheese

2 tablespoons fresh lemon juice

2 cloves garlic, minced

1 teaspoon Dijon mustard

1 teaspoon Worcestershire sauce

¼ teaspoon fish sauce

¼ teaspoon fine sea salt

¼ teaspoon ground black pepper

FOR THE SALAD

2 large heads romaine lettuce, cored and finely shredded

1 to 2 cups croutons

½ cup freshly shaved, grated, or shredded Parmesan cheese

½ cup shelled sunflower seeds

Fine sea salt, to taste

Ground black pepper, to taste

1 In a small, wide-mouth mason jar, combine all of the dressing ingredients and blend using an immersion blender until smooth.

2 In a large bowl, layer the romaine lettuce, croutons, Parmesan cheese, and sunflower seeds.

3 Drizzle the salad with the dressing and toss. Season with salt and pepper as needed. Refrigerate until ready to serve.

Chinese-Style Cucumber Salad

We've had an abundance of cucumbers in our garden the last couple years, so I've become pretty handy at turning them into tasty treats! This East Asian–inspired salad is one of our favorite ways to eat cucumbers. It pairs nicely with the Curry Chicken Stir-Fry (page 172) or is beautiful on its own.

Serves 2 to 4

FOR THE DRESSING

2 tablespoons coconut aminos or low-sodium soy sauce

2 tablespoons peanut or almond butter

2 teaspoons toasted sesame oil

1 teaspoon rice vinegar

1 teaspoon sriracha

1 teaspoon raw honey

½ teaspoon fine sea salt

¼ teaspoon ground black pepper

FOR THE SALAD

6 mini cucumbers, thinly sliced

3 green onions, thinly sliced

1 In a medium bowl, combine all of the dressing ingredients and stir until smooth.

2 Add the cucumbers and green onions and toss until well coated. Let sit for 5 minutes before serving.

Thai Peanut Chicken Salad

This is a fantastic meal-prep or make-ahead recipe because it doesn't have anything that will wilt. In fact, it only becomes tastier the longer it sits! Pair it with chicken or a plant-based protein like quinoa. If you don't like making your own dressings and sauces, you can use ½ cup of your favorite store-bought peanut sauce instead. Store leftovers in an airtight container in the refrigerator for up to 5 days.

Serves 4

FOR THE DRESSING

¼ cup peanut butter

¼ cup rice vinegar

2 tablespoons coconut aminos or low-sodium soy sauce

2 tablespoons sriracha or red chili sauce

2 green onions, finely chopped

1 teaspoon fine sea salt

¼ teaspoon onion powder

FOR THE SALAD

1 pound boneless, skinless chicken breasts, cooked and shredded

3 cups shredded red and/or green cabbage

2 cups edamame beans

2 cups shredded carrots

1 red bell pepper, seeded and finely diced

¼ cup raw or lightly salted peanuts (optional)

1 In a small, wide-mouth mason jar, combine all of the dressing ingredients and blend using an immersion blender until smooth.

2 In a large bowl, combine the chicken, cabbage, edamame, carrots, bell pepper, and peanuts (if using).

3 Top with the dressing and toss until combined.

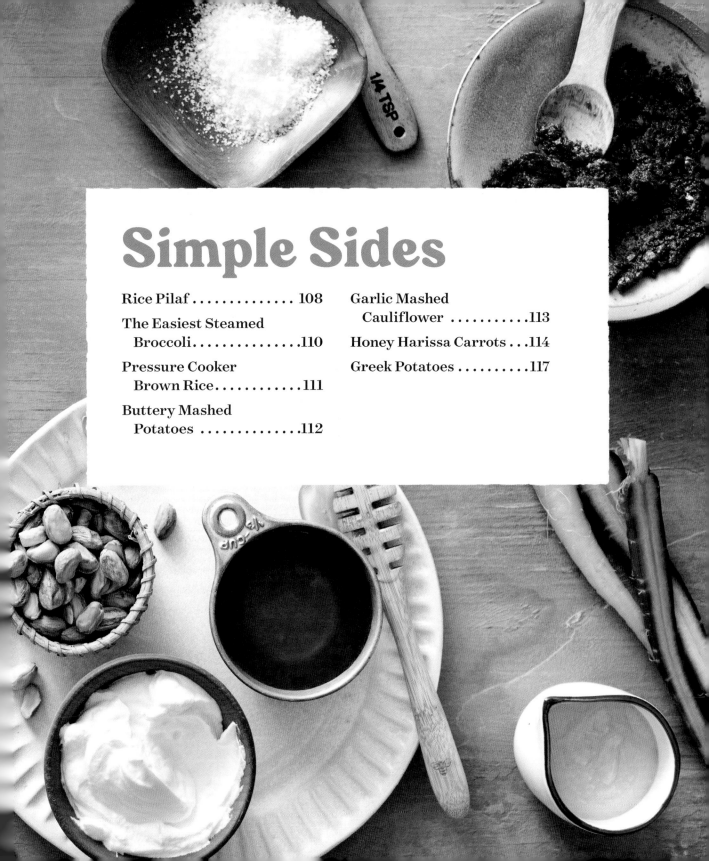

Simple Sides

Rice Pilaf 108

The Easiest Steamed
   Broccoli 110

Pressure Cooker
   Brown Rice 111

Buttery Mashed
   Potatoes 112

Garlic Mashed
   Cauliflower 113

Honey Harissa Carrots . . . 114

Greek Potatoes 117

Rice Pilaf

This is a simple Persian dish with rice, vegetables, and spices. Nearly every region in the world has a variation. Most are made with wheat or bulgur, but I like to use a gluten-free orzo. Jovial is my favorite brand; it is made with cassava flour.

Serves 4

¼ cup extra-virgin olive oil

⅓ cup gluten-free orzo

1 teaspoon garlic powder

1 teaspoon dried parsley

¾ teaspoon fine sea salt

¼ teaspoon ground black pepper

¼ teaspoon onion powder

¼ teaspoon paprika

2 cups frozen mixed vegetables

1 cup white rice

1½ cups chicken broth, homemade (page 243) or store-bought

1 Preheat an electric pressure cooker using the **SAUTÉ** function.

2 When the display panel reads **HOT**, add the olive oil, orzo, garlic powder, parsley, salt, pepper, onion powder, and paprika. Cook, stirring occasionally, for 2 to 3 minutes, or until browned.

3 Add the frozen vegetables, rice, and broth.

4 Place the lid on the cooker and make sure the vent valve is in the **SEALING** position. Select the **MANUAL/ PRESSURE COOK** function and **HIGH PRESSURE**. Use the +/- buttons until the display reads 3 minutes.

5 When the cooker beeps, let it naturally release the pressure, about 14 minutes.

6 Serve warm.

The Easiest Steamed Broccoli

This is literally the easiest way to get a side of greens on your plate. I started using this method a couple years ago and I've never looked back. Perfectly steamed broccoli every time! Change it up by adding lemon juice, oil, or different seasonings.

Serves 2

1 pound broccoli florets

4 cups water

1 teaspoon fine sea salt

½ teaspoon ground black pepper

1   Put the broccoli in a large, heat-safe glass bowl.

2   Bring the water to a boil in an electric kettle or small saucepan over high heat.

3   Pour the boiling water over the broccoli, then cover the bowl with aluminum foil.

4   Let the broccoli steam for 5 minutes, then drain in a colander.

5   Return the broccoli to the bowl and toss with the salt and pepper.

Pressure Cooker Brown Rice

This simple brown rice is a complex carbohydrate staple in my house! Soak the rice for 4 to 8 hours before cooking it to make it easier to digest or, if you don't have time, just make it according to the directions. I recommend adding scrambled eggs and mixed vegetables with a tablespoon of oil and coconut aminos for a delicious healthy spin on fried rice!

Serves 4

1½ cups water

1 cup short- or long-grain brown rice

½ teaspoon fine sea salt

½ teaspoon ground black pepper

1 In an electric pressure cooker, combine the water, rice, salt, and pepper.

2 Place the lid on the pressure cooker and make sure the vent valve is in the **SEALING** position. Select the **MANUAL/PRESSURE COOK** function and **HIGH PRESSURE**. Use the +/– buttons until the display reads 28 minutes.

3 When the cooker beeps, switch the vent valve from the **SEALING** to the **VENTING** position. Use caution while the steam escapes.

4 Serve warm.

Buttery Mashed Potatoes

This is an excellent and versatile dish because you can combine it with other recipes. For instance, say you want to make the Swedish Meatballs on page 195—just add the potatoes to the pot with the meatballs, remove the potatoes after cooking, and mash them with the salt and ghee. You can add them to other recipes with cook times ranging from 8 to 40 minutes.

Serves 4

½ cup chicken broth, homemade (page 243) or store-bought

4 red potatoes, quartered

½ teaspoon fine sea salt

1 tablespoon ghee

1 In an electric pressure cooker, combine the broth and potatoes.

2 Place the lid on the pressure cooker and make sure the vent valve is in the **SEALING** position. Select the **MANUAL/PRESSURE COOK** function and **HIGH PRESSURE**. Use the +/- buttons until the display reads 15 minutes.

3 When the cooker beeps, switch the vent valve from the **SEALING** to the **VENTING** position. Use caution while the steam escapes.

4 Transfer the potatoes to a large bowl. Add the salt and ghee and use an immersion blender to blend until smooth and creamy. Serve warm.

Garlic Mashed Cauliflower

I rebelled against the idea of using cauliflower as a substitute for mashed potatoes for quite some time. I guess I needed to heed that age-old advice, "Don't knock it 'til you've tried it." This simple cauliflower mash is a more than acceptable substitute for mashed spuds if you're trying to keep your starchy vegetables to a minimum.

Serves 2 to 4

1 cup water

1 large head cauliflower, cored and cut into large florets

1 teaspoon fine sea salt

½ teaspoon garlic powder

1   Pour the water into an electric pressure cooker. Place a trivet or steamer basket inside. Put the cauliflower on the trivet.

2   Place the lid on the cooker and make sure the vent valve is in the **SEALING** position. Select the **MANUAL/PRESSURE COOK** function and **HIGH PRESSURE**. Use the +/- buttons until the display reads 3 minutes.

3   When the cooker beeps, switch the vent valve from the **SEALING** to the **VENTING** position. Use caution while the steam escapes.

4   Drain the cauliflower in a colander, then transfer to a medium bowl. Stir in the salt and garlic powder. Using an immersion blender, blend until smooth. Serve warm.

Honey Harissa Carrots

Harissa is a hot chili pepper paste commonly used in Middle Eastern and North African cooking. I buy the Trader Joe's brand, but other brands can be found in most supermarkets. You can make your own tahini or buy it, but keep in mind that different brands vary in consistency. If your tahini is on the thicker side, add a little water to the sauce to thin it out and make it more drizzleable.

Serves 4

1 pound carrots, washed and trimmed

1 cup plus 2 tablespoons water

¼ cup Greek yogurt or dairy-free yogurt of choice

2 tablespoons tahini, homemade (page 239) or store-bought

1½ teaspoons harissa paste

½ teaspoon fine sea salt

¼ teaspoon ground black pepper

½ cup roasted pistachios, roughly chopped

2 tablespoons raw honey

1 If any of the carrots are large, cut them in half crosswise, then cut the fatter end in half lengthwise. You want all the carrot pieces to be more or less uniform.

2 In an electric pressure cooker, combine the carrots and 1 cup of the water.

3 Place the lid on the cooker and make sure the vent valve is in the **SEALING** position. Select the **MANUAL/ PRESSURE COOK** function and **HIGH PRESSURE**. Use the +/- buttons until the display reads 4 minutes.

4 In a small bowl, whisk together the yogurt, tahini, remaining 2 tablespoons water, and harissa until smooth.

5 When the cooker beeps, switch the vent valve from the **SEALING** to the **VENTING** position. Use caution while the steam escapes.

6 Drain the carrots in a colander, then transfer to a platter. Season with the salt and pepper. Spoon the harissa sauce over the carrots and sprinkle with the pistachios. Drizzle the honey over the top and serve warm.

Greek Potatoes

Crispy on the outside and creamy on the inside—this is one of my favorite ways to cook potatoes! If you'd prefer to use an air fryer, cook the potatoes in batches at 400°F for 20 to 25 minutes, turning halfway through.

Serves 6

3 pounds baby gold potatoes, quartered

⅓ cup extra-virgin olive oil

½ cup chicken broth, homemade (page 243) or store-bought

Grated zest and juice of 1 lemon

2 teaspoons dried oregano

1 teaspoon fine sea salt

½ teaspoon ground black pepper

½ teaspoon garlic powder

3 tablespoons fresh parsley leaves

1 Preheat the oven to 400°F.

2 In a large bowl, combine the potatoes, olive oil, broth, lemon zest and juice, oregano, salt, pepper, and garlic powder and toss well. Transfer the potatoes to a large rimmed baking sheet and spread out in a single layer.

3 Bake for 20 minutes. Turn the potatoes over and continue baking for an additional 25 to 30 minutes, or until fork-tender and golden brown.

4 Sprinkle with the parsley and serve.

Meatless Mains

Edamame Pesto Rotini . . 120

Roasted Eggplant with
Lemon-Dill Tahini and
Paprika Vinaigrette . . . 123

Coconut Red Lentil Dal
with Spinach 124

The Best-Ever Cabbage
Soup 126

Pulled BBQ Mushrooms
on Toast 127

Creamy Jamaican-Style
Pasta with Jerk
Mushrooms 128

Jollof Rice with
Red Beans 130

Carrot Dogs 133

Ground Tofu Tacos 134

Sesame Peanut Noodles
with Edamame
and Greens 136

Bean and Rice Burritos . . 137

Edamame Pesto Rotini

This is such a simple but satisfying pasta dish. Lean and green with edamame for protein, it's one that kids and parents alike adore. Try adding a handful or two of spinach to the pesto for more veggies. Sometimes I roast cherry tomatoes in my air fryer at 370°F for 10 to 15 minutes and add them at the end for a mildly acidic punch.

Serves 4

2 cups packed fresh basil leaves, plus more for garnish

⅓ cup pine nuts

1 tablespoon nutritional yeast

2 tablespoons extra-virgin olive oil

3 cloves garlic, peeled

1 teaspoon fine sea salt

½ teaspoon ground black pepper

12 ounces gluten-free rotini, cooked according to package instructions and drained

1½ cups shelled edamame

1 In a food processor, combine the basil, pine nuts, nutritional yeast, olive oil, garlic, salt, and pepper. Blend until smooth; this may require slowly drizzling in additional olive oil while the machine is running.

2 In a large bowl, combine the pasta, edamame, and pesto and toss. Top with fresh basil and serve warm.

Roasted Eggplant with Lemon-Dill Tahini and Paprika Vinaigrette

This light and refreshing dinner can pair with a meat protein or simple salad, or be eaten by itself. I usually have a little bit of the tahini dressing left over—what a delight! It's good paired with other vegetables, used as the base for a potato salad, or drizzled over a fresh garden salad. Stored in an airtight jar in the refrigerator, it will last for weeks!

If you do not have an air fryer, you can bake the eggplant in the oven at 475°F for 20 minutes, flipping it over halfway through.

Serves 2

FOR THE EGGPLANT

1 medium eggplant, peeled and sliced into 1-inch rounds

3 tablespoons extra-virgin olive oil

½ teaspoon fine sea salt

½ teaspoon ground black pepper

FOR THE LEMON-DILL TAHINI DRESSING

½ cup tahini, homemade (page 239) or store-bought

Juice of 2 lemons

¼ cup finely chopped fresh dill

3 cloves garlic, minced

1 teaspoon fine sea salt

¼ to ½ cup cold water

FOR THE PAPRIKA VINAIGRETTE

1 tablespoon extra-virgin olive oil

1½ teaspoons white vinegar

1 clove garlic, minced

½ teaspoon paprika

¼ teaspoon garlic powder

¼ teaspoon fine sea salt

¼ teaspoon ground black pepper

1 Spread out the eggplant slices on a cutting board. Brush each side with the olive oil and season with the salt and pepper.

2 Working in batches, arrange the eggplant slices in the basket of a 5.3-quart air fryer and cook at 400°F for 18 minutes, turning halfway through.

3 While the eggplant cooks, in a medium bowl, whisk together all of the tahini ingredients, adding the water little by little until the dressing is spreadable but not runny.

4 In a smaller bowl, whisk together all of the ingredients for the paprika vinaigrette.

5 When the eggplant has finished cooking, top with the tahini dressing and drizzle with the paprika vinaigrette. Serve warm.

Coconut Red Lentil Dal with Spinach

This traditional Indian dish is packed full of flavor. It's vegan and protein-rich and so easy to make! I like to serve it with rice, but it's also delicious over fresh naan or quinoa. You can find the cooking times for both on page 22.

Serves 4 to 6

FOR THE DAL

1½ cups red lentils

1 medium yellow onion, finely diced

1 large carrot, diced

4 cloves garlic, minced

1 tablespoon grated fresh ginger

3 cups vegetable broth, homemade (page 244) or store-bought

1 (14.5-ounce) can diced tomatoes with juices

¾ cup canned full-fat coconut milk

1 tablespoon garam masala, homemade (page 236) or store-bought

1 tablespoon curry powder

½ teaspoon fine sea salt

FOR SERVING

3 cups packed baby spinach

2 to 3 cups cooked rice of choice (see page 22)

1 In an electric pressure cooker, combine all of the dal ingredients.

2 Place the lid on the pressure cooker and make sure the vent valve is in the **SEALING** position. Select the **MANUAL/PRESSURE COOK** function and **HIGH PRESSURE**. Use the +/- buttons until the display reads 10 minutes.

3 When the cooker beeps, let it naturally release the pressure until the display reads **LO:05**. Switch the vent valve from the **SEALING** to the **VENTING** position. Use caution while the steam escapes.

4 Stir in the spinach until it wilts and serve over the rice.

The Best-Ever Cabbage Soup

I could eat this soup every day. The flavors are bold and, really, just spectacular. It's also brimming with essential nutrients. Forget one bowl, eat two! And make extra because you'll for sure want to pack it for lunch tomorrow.

Serves 6

2 tablespoons extra-virgin olive oil

1 large yellow onion, diced

2 cups diced carrots

2 cups diced celery

1½ teaspoons minced garlic

½ medium to large head green cabbage, cored and chopped

2 tablespoons fresh parsley, plus more for garnish

1 (15-ounce) can great northern beans, rinsed and drained

1 (14.5-ounce) can diced tomatoes with juices

2 cups vegetable broth, homemade (page 244) or store-bought

1 cup water

1 teaspoon chili powder

1 teaspoon dried thyme

1½ teaspoons fine sea salt

½ to 1 teaspoon ground black pepper

⅛ teaspoon red pepper flakes

Lemon wedges, for serving (optional)

1 Preheat an electric pressure cooker using the **SAUTÉ** function.

2 When the display panel reads **HOT**, add the olive oil, onion, carrots, and celery. Cook, stirring occasionally, until the onion is translucent, about 5 minutes. Stir in the garlic and cook for 1 minute.

3 Add the cabbage, parsley, beans, tomatoes, broth, water, chili powder, thyme, salt, black pepper, and red pepper flakes and stir to combine.

4 Place the lid on the cooker and make sure the vent valve is in the **SEALING** position. Select the **MANUAL/PRESSURE COOK** function and **HIGH PRESSURE**. Use the +/- buttons until the display reads 5 minutes.

5 When the cooker beeps, let it naturally release the pressure until the display reads **LO:05**. Switch the vent valve from the **SEALING** to the **VENTING** position. Use caution while the steam escapes.

6 Garnish with fresh parsley and serve warm with lemon wedges, if desired.

Pulled BBQ Mushrooms on Toast

Oyster mushrooms are delicate and soft and can be pulled apart to give a shredded appearance, but any variety of mushrooms can be cut into pieces for this recipe. This is fun to serve as an open-faced sandwich but also makes a great veggie burger on a bun.

Serves 1

FOR THE SLAW

1½ cups finely shredded green cabbage

1½ tablespoons mayonnaise, homemade (page 240) or store-bought

1 tablespoon apple cider vinegar

1 teaspoon 100% pure maple syrup

¼ teaspoon fine sea salt

⅛ teaspoon ground black pepper

FOR THE MUSHROOMS

1 tablespoon extra-virgin olive oil

4 ounces oyster mushrooms, pulled apart into strips

¼ teaspoon garlic powder

2 tablespoons barbecue sauce, homemade (page 241) or store-bought

2 slices bread of choice, toasted

1   In a medium bowl, toss together all of the slaw ingredients. Cover and refrigerate until ready to serve.

2   In a small saucepan, heat the oil over high heat. Add the mushrooms and garlic powder and sauté, stirring occasionally, until the mushrooms are wilted down, about 2 minutes. Turn the heat down to low and stir in the barbecue sauce. Allow to cook for another minute or so until the sauce thickens and coats the mushrooms.

3   Place the pieces of toast on a plate. Divide the mushrooms on top of each piece.

4   Stir the slaw and divide evenly on top of the mushrooms.

Creamy Jamaican-Style Pasta with Jerk Mushrooms

This is a Caribbean-inspired recipe with colorful peppers and jerk seasoning. The dish is as flexible as it is tasty—you can replace the mushrooms with a protein, if you prefer, like chicken or shrimp. You can also use any variety of pasta. This version is lighter and a tad sweeter (because of the coconut milk) than traditional recipes, but it's just as flavorful.

Serves 4

3 tablespoons extra-virgin olive oil

2 tablespoons jerk seasoning, homemade (page 237) or store-bought

1 pound portobello mushrooms or mushrooms of choice, stemmed and cut into ½-inch pieces

1 medium orange bell pepper, seeded and thinly sliced

1 medium green bell pepper, seeded and thinly sliced

1 small red onion, thinly sliced

½ cup diced tomato

4 cloves garlic, minced

½ cup vegetable broth, homemade (page 244) or store-bought

½ cup canned full-fat coconut milk

12 ounces gluten-free penne, cooked according to package instructions and drained

½ cup freshly grated Parmesan cheese

1 In a large bowl, combine 2 tablespoons of the oil and 1 tablespoon of the jerk seasoning. Add the mushrooms and toss well so the seasoning is evenly distributed.

2 Preheat an electric pressure cooker using the **SAUTÉ** function.

3 When the display panel reads **HOT**, add the mushrooms. Cook, stirring occasionally, for 3 minutes. Add the remaining 1 tablespoon oil, the 1 tablespoon remaining jerk seasoning, bell peppers, and onion and cook, stirring occasionally, until the onion is translucent, about 5 minutes.

4 Add the tomato, garlic, broth, and coconut milk.

5 Place the lid on the cooker and make sure the vent valve is in the **SEALING** position. Select the **MANUAL/PRESSURE COOK** function and **HIGH PRESSURE**. Use the +/- buttons until the display reads 5 minutes.

6 When the cooker beeps, let it naturally release the pressure until the display reads **LO:05**. Switch the vent valve from the **SEALING** to the **VENTING** position. Use caution while the steam escapes.

7 Stir in the pasta and Parmesan. Let the pasta sit for 5 minutes with the lid on before serving.

Jollof Rice with Red Beans

Jollof rice is a traditional dish from West Africa. It usually consists of tomato, onion, bell pepper, spices, and rice. For added protein, you can add 1½ pounds boneless, skinless chicken breast, cut into ½-inch pieces, to the pot with the rice and beans.

Serves 4

1 large tomato, roughly chopped

1 large jalapeño, roughly chopped

½ medium yellow onion, roughly chopped

1 red bell pepper, seeded and roughly chopped

3 cloves garlic, peeled

2 tablespoons tomato paste

2 tablespoons extra-virgin olive oil

1 teaspoon fine sea salt

¼ teaspoon cayenne pepper

1½ cups long-grain brown rice

1 (15-ounce) can red kidney beans, rinsed and drained

2 tablespoons chopped fresh parsley

1 In a high-powered blender, combine the tomato, jalapeño, onion, bell pepper, garlic, tomato paste, olive oil, salt, and cayenne. Blend on high for 1 minute, or until smooth.

2 Transfer the blended sauce to an electric pressure cooker and add the rice and beans.

3 Place the lid on the cooker and make sure the vent valve is in the **SEALING** position. Select the **MANUAL/ PRESSURE COOK** function and **HIGH PRESSURE**. Use the +/- buttons until the display reads 28 minutes.

4 When the cooker beeps, let it naturally release the pressure until the display reads **LO:10**. Switch the vent valve from the **SEALING** to the **VENTING** position. Use caution while the steam escapes.

5 Stir in the parsley and serve warm.

Carrot Dogs

This is such a fun plant-based spin on an all-American classic! I'm not against a good hot dog, but many brands are chock-full of less than stellar ingredients, and the healthier-for-you dogs tend to come with a less-than-healthy price tag. So, here's a fun alternative—I beg you, don't knock it till you try it!

Serves 6

6 large or extra-large carrots, cut in half lengthwise

¼ cup coconut aminos or low-sodium soy sauce

¼ cup apple cider vinegar

¼ cup vegetable broth, homemade (page 244) or store-bought

2 tablespoons pickled jalapeño juice

2 tablespoons 100% pure maple syrup

1 tablespoon liquid smoke

2 teaspoons yellow mustard

½ teaspoon garlic powder

1 teaspoon onion powder

6 hot dog buns

Ketchup, mustard, and relish, for serving

¼ cup diced onion

1 In an electric pressure cooker, combine the carrots, coconut aminos, vinegar, broth, pickled jalapeño juice, maple syrup, liquid smoke, mustard, garlic powder, and onion powder.

2 Place the lid on the pressure cooker and make sure the vent valve is in the **SEALING** position. Select the **MANUAL/PRESSURE COOK** function and **HIGH PRESSURE**. Use the +/- buttons until the display reads 8 minutes.

3 When the cooker beeps, switch the vent valve from the **SEALING** to the **VENTING** position. Use caution while the steam escapes.

4 Remove the carrots from the cooker and place inside the buns. Top with ketchup, mustard, relish, and diced onion. Serve warm.

Ground Tofu Tacos

This tofu tastes just like taco meat—I guarantee you won't be able to tell the difference! I love tacos because they're such a blank slate; you can do them really bare-bones or add all kinds of veggies and dress them up. I like to use cabbage, onion, fresh herbs—anything I have that needs to be used up. You can also add diced bell peppers, jalapeños, potatoes, and/or mushrooms to the tofu bake. Make these in a bowl if you're trying to limit your starchy carbohydrate intake.

Serves 4

2 tablespoons extra-virgin olive oil, plus more for greasing

1 (16-ounce) package extra-firm tofu, drained, sliced, pressed dry, and crumbled

3 tablespoons coconut aminos or low-sodium soy sauce

1 teaspoon garlic powder

1 teaspoon onion powder

1 teaspoon ground cumin

1 teaspoon chili powder

2 tablespoons nutritional yeast

8 corn tortilla shells

1 head romaine lettuce, cored and shredded

2 Roma tomatoes, diced

Favorite hot sauce or salsa, for serving

1   Preheat the oven to 400°F. Lightly coat a rimmed baking sheet with oil.

2   In a large bowl, combine the crumbled tofu, coconut aminos, olive oil, garlic powder, onion powder, cumin, chili powder, and nutritional yeast. Mix until the tofu is completely coated.

3   Spread out the tofu on the prepared baking sheet and bake for 20 to 25 minutes.

4   Serve warm in tortilla shells topped with romaine, tomato, and your favorite hot sauce or salsa.

Sesame Peanut Noodles with Edamame and Greens

These peanut noodles come together quickly and can be made in under 10 minutes! Deliciously tangy and delightfully yummy, this slurpy noodle dish is a perfect complement to any day.

Fresh ginger pro tip: Buy a large knob of ginger and store it in a ziplock bag in your freezer! It'll keep for 6 months and you'll have it on hand anytime you need to grate it or toss it in a smoothie.

Serves 3

FOR THE NOODLES

1½ cups water

1 teaspoon fine sea salt

1 teaspoon grated fresh ginger

2 cloves garlic, minced

8 ounces pad thai rice noodles, broken into thirds

1 medium bunch bok choy, chopped

1 medium carrot, shredded

½ medium red bell pepper, seeded and diced

1 cup shelled edamame

½ cup chopped peanuts

2 green onions, thinly sliced (optional)

1 tablespoon sesame seeds (optional)

FOR THE SAUCE

2 tablespoons peanut butter

2 tablespoons coconut aminos or low-sodium soy sauce

1 tablespoon toasted sesame oil

1 tablespoon rice vinegar

1 tablespoon raw honey

1½ teaspoons sriracha

½ cup water

1   In an electric pressure cooker, combine the water, salt, ginger, and garlic. Add the rice noodles, bok choy, carrot, bell pepper, edamame, and peanuts. Do *not* stir.

2   Place the lid on the cooker and make sure the vent valve is in the **SEALING** position. Select the **MANUAL/PRESSURE COOK** function and **HIGH PRESSURE**. Use the +/- buttons until the display reads 6 minutes.

3   Meanwhile, in a small bowl, whisk together all of the sauce ingredients. Set aside.

4   When the cooker beeps, switch the vent valve from the **SEALING** to the **VENTING** position. Use caution while the steam escapes.

5   Stir in the sauce and serve hot, topped with the green onions and sesame seeds, if desired.

Bean and Rice Burritos

When I was younger, after a late night of football practice or theater, we'd usually stop on the way home at Del Taco or Taco Bell and grab bean and cheese burritos. I'll still get a taste for a delicious burrito while on the go, but now I make my own burritos ahead of time. I've taken these on road trips, through airports, and to amusement parks. They freeze great and are a perfect make-ahead lunch to bring to school or work. Just wrap them in a piece of parchment paper so they stay individual and enjoy!

Serves 6

1 tablespoon extra-virgin olive oil

1¼ cups chicken broth, homemade (page 243) or store-bought, or water

1 cup brown rice

1 (15-ounce) can pinto beans, rinsed and drained

1 (14.5-ounce) can diced tomatoes with juices

1 (4-ounce) can green chiles

1½ tablespoons chili powder

1 tablespoon ground cumin

1½ teaspoons fine sea salt

1 teaspoon garlic powder

1 teaspoon dried minced onion or onion powder

1 teaspoon paprika

1 teaspoon dried oregano

½ teaspoon cayenne pepper (optional)

1 cup sour cream

6 large corn tortillas

1 cup shredded Mexican blend cheese (optional)

1 head romaine lettuce, cored and shredded

Hot sauce of choice, for serving

Butter, for frying (optional)

1 In an electric pressure cooker, combine the olive oil, broth, rice, beans, tomatoes, green chiles, chili powder, cumin, salt, garlic powder, minced onion, paprika, oregano, and cayenne (if using).

2 Place the lid on the cooker and make sure the vent valve is in the **SEALING** position. Select the **MANUAL/PRESSURE COOK** function and **HIGH PRESSURE**. Use the +/- buttons until the display reads 28 minutes.

3 When the cooker beeps, switch the vent valve from the **SEALING** to the **VENTING** position. Use caution while the steam escapes.

4 Layer some sour cream and the rice mixture on each tortilla. Top with some cheese (if using), lettuce, and hot sauce and roll up. Serve as is or heat some butter in a large cast-iron skillet over medium heat and pan-fry the burritos.

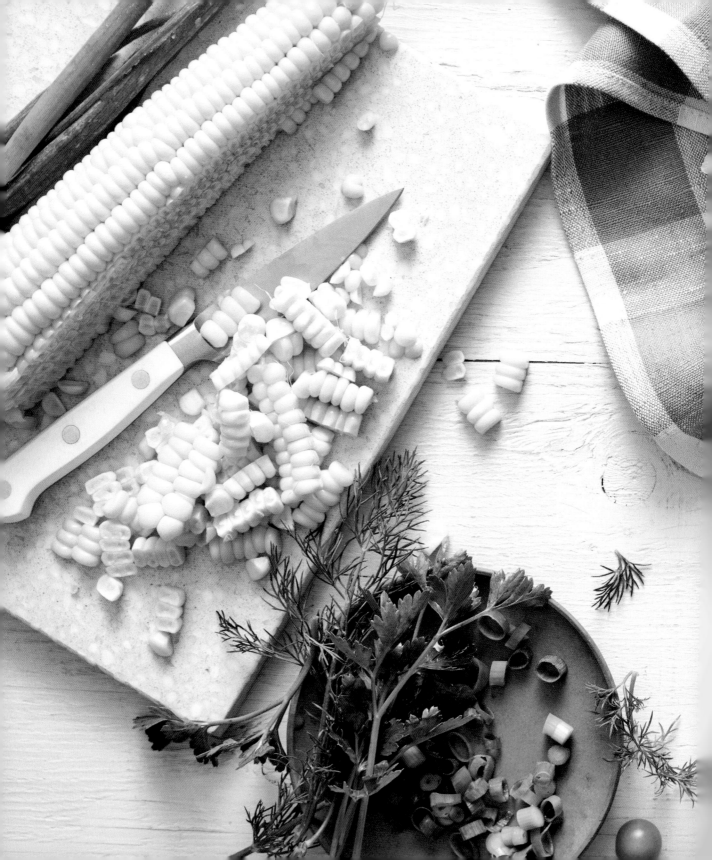

Recipes for One

Red Chile Tostada 140

Pepperoni Zucchini
  Pizza 141

Zesty Herby Corn and
  Cucumber Salad 142

Lightened-Up Turkey
  Reuben 144

Teriyaki Salmon
  Rice Bowls 146

Bang Bang Chicken 149

Red Chile Tostada

This is a great quick lunch or breakfast that takes just 10 minutes to make. It is full of fiber, protein, and healthy fats that will keep you feeling fuller longer! I eat one if I'm having a smoothie or green juice on the side or two if it's the only thing I'm eating for a meal. Feel free to add pico de gallo, sliced avocado or guacamole, chopped fresh Roma tomatoes, and/or shredded romaine lettuce to really jazz it up!

Serves 1

1 tablespoon avocado oil

1 corn tortilla

2 tablespoons hot sauce or enchilada sauce

1 large egg

Fine sea salt, to taste

Ground black pepper, to taste

2 tablespoons canned refried black beans

1 tablespoon chopped fresh cilantro (optional)

1 Heat the oil in a cast-iron skillet over medium-high heat. Add the tortilla and let the bottom absorb a little oil, then flip it over so the other side can absorb the rest. Let each side cook until crispy, 3 to 5 minutes on each side. Remove from the heat and place it on a paper towel to absorb the excess oil.

2 Turn the heat down to medium-low. Working quickly, add 1 tablespoon of the hot sauce to the pan and crack the egg on top of the sauce. Sprinkle the top of the egg with a little salt and pepper. Once the bottom has fried, about 3 minutes, flip it over and cook to your preferred doneness.

3 Spread the crispy tortilla with the refried beans. Top with the egg and remaining 1 tablespoon hot sauce, then sprinkle with the cilantro (if using). Serve immediately.

Pepperoni Zucchini Pizza

Mmmmm, this recipe is a real family pleaser—just scale the recipe up to make as many as you need for a quick and delicious meal! I like to use Rao's marinara or Simply Nature organic tomato and basil sauce from Aldi. If pepperoni isn't your jam, these can be made into three-cheese Alfredo pizzas, using Alfredo Sauce (page 191), shredded mozzarella, and grated Parmesan. You can also pack it full of your favorite sautéed veggies to make a veggie-on-veggie pizza! The sky's the limit.

Serves 1

2 medium zucchinis

½ teaspoon Italian seasoning, homemade (page 238) or store-bought

½ teaspoon fine sea salt

¼ teaspoon ground black pepper

⅔ cup marinara sauce

¼ cup shredded mozzarella cheese

1 ounce nitrate-free sliced pepperonis

1 Cut the ends off each zucchini, then cut them in half lengthwise. Scoop out the seeds.

2 Sprinkle the zucchini halves with the Italian seasoning, salt, and pepper. Spoon in the marinara sauce, top with half of the mozzarella, add the pepperonis, and then sprinkle with the remaining mozzarella.

3 Place the stuffed zucchinis in a 5.3-quart air-fryer basket and bake at 370°F for 8 to 10 minutes.

4 Serve immediately.

Zesty Herby Corn and Cucumber Salad

Want to spice up your salad life? I've got just the recipe for you! This salad is delicious, tangy, packed full of herbs and veggies, and seriously satisfying! It's amazing on its own or paired with grilled chicken and corn tortilla chips.

Serves 1

½ cup frozen white or yellow corn kernels, warmed

¼ cup diced cherry tomatoes

¼ English cucumber, diced

2 green onions, chopped

½ head romaine lettuce, cored and thinly sliced

Juice of ½ lemon

1 tablespoon extra-virgin olive oil

1 tablespoon white vinegar

2 tablespoons finely chopped fresh dill

1 tablespoon finely chopped fresh parsley

1 clove garlic, finely chopped

¼ teaspoon onion powder

¼ teaspoon fine sea salt

Pinch ground black pepper

Combine all of the ingredients in a medium bowl and toss well.

Lightened-Up Turkey Reuben

I love a good sandwich, and this one won't disappoint! With five simple ingredients, it comes together quickly and is the perfect on-the-go lunch or late-night dinner.

Serves 1

2 tablespoons Thousand Island Dressing (recipe follows) or store-bought, plus more as needed

2 slices whole-grain rye or sourdough bread, toasted

2 large slices nitrate-free turkey breast

¼ cup sauerkraut, drained

1 thin slice Swiss cheese

1 Spread the dressing on both slices of the bread. Top one slice of bread with the sliced turkey, sauerkraut, and cheese, then place the second slice on top.

2 Place the sandwich in the basket of a 5.3-quart air fryer and cook at 360°F for 5 to 8 minutes, or until the cheese melts.

3 Add additional dressing, if desired, and serve warm.

Thousand Island Dressing

Drastically healthier than store-bought versions, this dressing is a great salad topper or a beautiful sandwich or burger spread!

Makes ¾ cup

½ cup sour cream or Greek yogurt

2 tablespoons ketchup

2 tablespoons pickle relish

1 teaspoon Worcestershire sauce

¾ teaspoon fine sea salt

¼ teaspoon ground black pepper

In a medium bowl, whisk together all of the ingredients. Store in an airtight container in the refrigerator for up to 1 week.

Teriyaki Salmon Rice Bowls

This yummy deconstructed sushi-esque bowl is a really fun and easy take on one of my favorite Japanese meals. I like to keep different cooked complex carbohydrates in the fridge each week to use as a base for these bowls—like sweet potato, brown rice, or lentils—any will work in this recipe!

Serves 1

1 (4.5-ounce) can wild-caught salmon, drained

1 tablespoon mayonnaise, homemade (page 240) or store-bought

1 tablespoon The Best Homemade Teriyaki Sauce (recipe follows)

2 green onions, chopped

Pinch fine sea salt

¾ cup cooked brown rice (see page 22)

½ cup diced Persian cucumber

Chopped nori, furikake, and sesame seeds, for topping (optional)

1 In a small bowl, combine the salmon, mayo, ½ tablespoon of the teriyaki sauce, the green onions, and salt. Mix well.

2 Put the rice in a separate bowl, top it with the prepared salmon and cucumber, and drizzle with the remaining ½ tablespoon teriyaki sauce. Garnish with nori, furikake, and sesame seeds, if desired.

The Best Homemade Teriyaki Sauce

Store-bought teriyaki sauces generally have copious amounts of added sugar and preservatives. It's so easy to make your own and barely takes any time at all. This amount is perfect to pair with 1 pound of chicken, fish, or tofu.

Makes ¼ cup

1 tablespoon raw honey

1 tablespoon sriracha

2 teaspoons coconut aminos or low-sodium soy sauce

1 teaspoon coconut sugar

1 teaspoon toasted sesame oil

½ teaspoon ground ginger

½ teaspoon garlic powder

In a small bowl, whisk together all of the ingredients. Store in an airtight container in the refrigerator for up to 1 week.

Bang Bang Chicken

Bang bang chicken is one of my favorite Chinese dishes. This lightened-up version is crispy but tender and coated in a thick, creamy sauce that is savory, spicy, and sweet all at once! You can substitute shrimp or portobello mushrooms for the chicken in this recipe—just cut the cook time in half.

Serves 1

FOR THE VEGGIES

1 small sweet potato, cut in half lengthwise, and sliced into ½-inch pieces

½ orange bell pepper, seeded and cut into large pieces

½ red onion, cut into 1-inch pieces

1½ teaspoons extra-virgin olive oil

½ teaspoon fine sea salt

¼ teaspoon black pepper

FOR THE SAUCE

2 tablespoons mayonnaise, homemade (page 240) or store-bought

1 teaspoon harissa paste

1 teaspoon raw honey

½ teaspoon apple cider vinegar

FOR THE CHICKEN

1 boneless, skinless chicken breast

½ teaspoon garlic powder

½ teaspoon fine sea salt

¼ teaspoon ground black pepper

1 teaspoon arrowroot powder

1 Preheat the oven to 425°F.

2 On a rimmed baking sheet, toss the sweet potato, bell pepper, and onion with the olive oil, salt, and pepper, then spread out in a single layer. Bake for 10 minutes.

3 Meanwhile, in a small bowl, whisk together all of the sauce ingredients. Set aside.

4 Cut ½-inch slits in the chicken breast about 1 inch apart. Do not slice all the way through. Sprinkle the chicken with the garlic powder, salt, pepper, and arrowroot powder. Brush 1 tablespoon of the sauce all over the chicken, making sure it gets into the slits.

5 Place the chicken on the baking sheet away from the vegetables. Bake for 20 minutes, or until the chicken reaches an internal temperature of 165°F. If the vegetables begin to get too dark, cover them with a piece of aluminum foil.

6 Transfer the vegetables to a plate and top with the chicken. Serve with the remaining sauce.

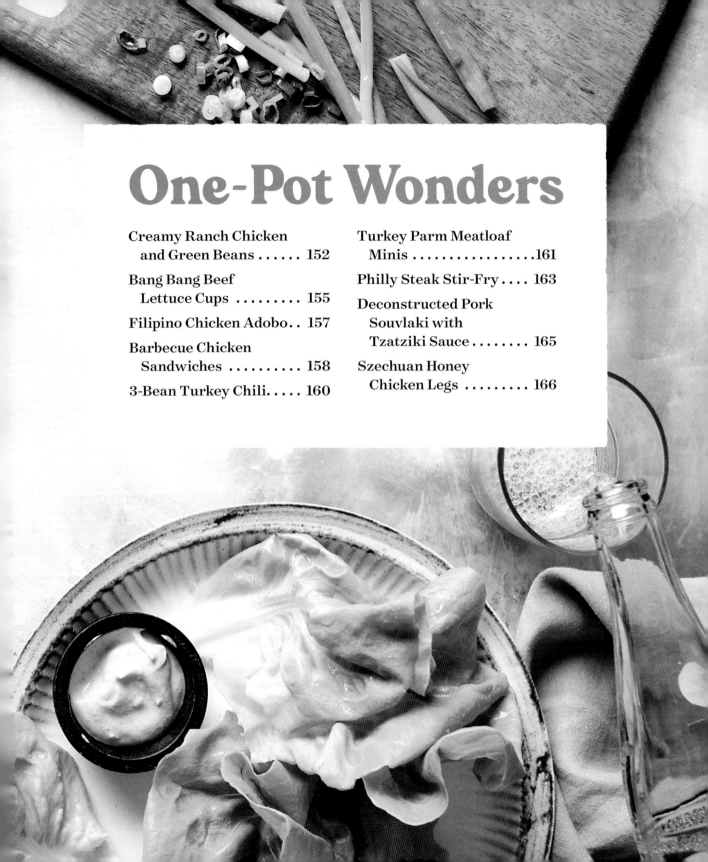

One-Pot Wonders

Creamy Ranch Chicken
and Green Beans 152

Bang Bang Beef
Lettuce Cups 155

Filipino Chicken Adobo. . 157

Barbecue Chicken
Sandwiches 158

3-Bean Turkey Chili. 160

Turkey Parm Meatloaf
Minis 161

Philly Steak Stir-Fry 163

Deconstructed Pork
Souvlaki with
Tzatziki Sauce 165

Szechuan Honey
Chicken Legs 166

Creamy Ranch Chicken and Green Beans

This zesty, tangy chicken is delicious paired with green beans, as I do here, or it makes an excellent addition to a salad! You can even serve it over a baked potato. I like to make it with my homemade ranch dressing, but Primal Kitchen, Noble Made, and Chef Hak's are fantastic alternatives.

Serves 4

1 pound boneless, skinless chicken breasts

1 pound frozen or fresh green beans

¼ cup chicken broth, homemade (page 243) or store-bought, or water

1 tablespoon apple cider vinegar

2 tablespoons chopped fresh chives

1 tablespoon dried parsley flakes

1 teaspoon garlic powder

1 teaspoon dried dill

1 teaspoon fine sea salt

½ teaspoon ground black pepper

½ cup Creamy Ranch Dressing, homemade (recipe follows) or store-bought

1   In an electric pressure cooker, combine all of the ingredients except the ranch dressing.

2   Place the lid on the pressure cooker and make sure the vent valve is in the **SEALING** position. Select the **MANUAL/PRESSURE COOK** function and **HIGH PRESSURE**. Use the +/- buttons until the display reads 30 minutes.

3   When the cooker beeps, let it naturally release the pressure until the display reads **LO:05**. Switch the vent valve from the **SEALING** to the **VENTING** position. Use caution while the steam escapes.

4   Remove the chicken from the cooker and cut into thin slices.

5   In a medium bowl, toss the chicken with the ranch dressing. Serve the chicken with the green beans on the side.

Creamy Ranch Dressing

Ranch lovers, this one's for you! This recipe has all the flavor of the original, but it's made with avocado oil instead of gut-irritating, processed seed oils and refined sugar. It's better for your blood sugar and your waistline.

Makes ¾ cup

¾ cup mayonnaise, homemade (page 240) or store-bought

1 teaspoon apple cider vinegar

1 teaspoon fresh lemon juice

1 teaspoon dried parsley flakes

1 teaspoon fine sea salt

½ teaspoon garlic powder

½ teaspoon onion powder

½ teaspoon dried dill

1 In a small, wide-mouth jar, combine all of the ingredients and blend with an immersion blender until smooth.

2 Store in an airtight container in the refrigerator for up to 1 week.

Bang Bang Beef Lettuce Cups

This 20-minute weeknight dinner is inspired by one of my favorite Chinese dishes and can be made in your electric pressure cooker or on the stovetop. It's only one pot, so don't worry about the cleanup! Leftovers are delicious over brown or jasmine rice—it's like an entirely new meal!

Serves 4 to 6

1½ teaspoons extra-virgin olive oil

1 medium yellow onion, finely chopped

4 cloves garlic, minced

1½ pounds grass-fed ground beef

¼ cup coconut aminos or low-sodium soy sauce

2 tablespoons rice vinegar

1½ tablespoons hoisin sauce

1 tablespoon toasted sesame oil

½ teaspoon ground ginger

¼ teaspoon fine sea salt

¼ teaspoon ground black pepper

½ cup shredded carrots

½ cup chopped water chestnuts

⅓ cup chopped green onions

1 head butterleaf lettuce, separated into leaves

1 recipe Bang Bang Sauce (recipe follows)

1 Preheat an electric pressure cooker using the **SAUTÉ** function and adjust the heat to **MORE**.

2 When the display panel reads **HOT**, add the olive oil, onion, garlic, and ground beef. Cook, stirring occasionally, until the onion has softened and the beef is about three-quarters of the way cooked, about 5 minutes. Add the coconut aminos, vinegar, hoisin sauce, sesame oil, ginger, salt, pepper, carrots, water chestnuts, and green onions and cook for 2 to 3 minutes.

3 Serve the beef in butterleaf lettuce "cups" and top with the sauce.

Bang Bang Sauce

This fantastic sauce, inspired by the traditional Chinese sauce, pairs well with the Bang Bang Beef Lettuce Cups (page 155) or grilled shrimp. I like to use Yai's Thai sweet chili sauce. It's delicious and Whole30 approved!

Makes ¾ cup

½ cup mayonnaise, homemade (page 240) or store-bought, or Greek yogurt

1 to 2 tablespoons sriracha

1½ teaspoons sweet chili sauce

1 teaspoon coconut aminos or low-sodium soy sauce

½ teaspoon rice vinegar

½ teaspoon garlic powder

⅛ teaspoon fine sea salt

⅛ teaspoon ground black pepper

Combine all of the ingredients in a medium bowl. Store in an airtight container in the refrigerator for up to 6 days.

Filipino Chicken Adobo

This is the national dish of the Philippines. I remember the first time I had it in middle school at a friend's house. It's known for its tangy and intensely flavorful sauce—a delicate balance of salt, sour, and sweet.

Serves 4

2 pounds boneless, skinless chicken thighs

½ cup coconut aminos or low-sodium soy sauce

¼ cup white vinegar

1 small yellow onion, finely diced

4 cloves garlic, minced

2 bay leaves

½ teaspoon red pepper flakes

2 tablespoons raw honey

4 cups cooked rice of choice (see page 22)

2 green onions, thinly sliced

1 In a ziplock bag, combine the chicken, coconut aminos, vinegar, onion, garlic, bay leaves, red pepper flakes, and honey. Marinate in the refrigerator for at least 1 hour or overnight.

2 Transfer the chicken and the marinade to an electric pressure cooker.

3 Place the lid on the cooker and make sure the vent valve is in the **SEALING** position. Select the **MANUAL/PRESSURE COOK** function and **HIGH PRESSURE**. Use the +/- buttons until the display reads 16 minutes.

4 When the cooker beeps, switch the vent valve from the **SEALING** to the **VENTING** position. Use caution while the steam escapes.

5 Press the **CANCEL** button and then select the **SAUTÉ** function. Allow the sauce to reduce for 3 minutes. Remove the bay leaves. Serve the chicken over the rice and top with the green onions.

Barbecue Chicken Sandwiches

This barbecue chicken recipe is so versatile—it can be used for sandwiches, sliders, salad, or served as is with a side of green beans and coleslaw! If you are not making your own barbecue sauce, I recommend Kinder's organic BBQ sauce.

Serves 4

1 pound boneless, skinless chicken breasts

½ cup barbecue sauce, homemade (page 241) or store-bought

2 tablespoons Classic Italian Dressing, homemade (page 246) or store-bought

2 tablespoons chicken broth, homemade (page 243) or store-bought

2 tablespoons coconut sugar

1½ teaspoons Worcestershire sauce

1 teaspoon fine sea salt

½ teaspoon ground black pepper

2 tablespoons mayonnaise, homemade (page 240) or store-bought

8 slices whole-grain, sourdough, or other sturdy bread of choice

½ head romaine lettuce, cored

2 Roma tomatoes, sliced thinly

½ cup sauerkraut

1 In an electric pressure cooker, combine the chicken, barbecue sauce, Italian dressing, broth, coconut sugar, Worcestershire sauce, salt, and pepper.

2 Place the lid on the pressure cooker and make sure the vent valve is in the **SEALING** position. Select the **MANUAL/PRESSURE COOK** function and **HIGH PRESSURE**. Use the +/- buttons until the display reads 16 minutes.

3 When the cooker beeps, let it naturally release the pressure until the display reads **LO:05**. Switch the vent valve from the **SEALING** to the **VENTING** position. Use caution while the steam escapes.

4 Shred the chicken into the juices with two forks and stir to combine.

5 Spread the mayo on each slice of bread. Top 4 slices with shredded chicken, lettuce leaves, tomato slices, and sauerkraut, then top with the other 4 slices. Serve warm.

3-Bean Turkey Chili

Talk about comfort food—there's nothing quite like a big pot of chili. This tasty turkey chili is packed with protein and fiber that will keep you feeling full and satisfied. It makes for great leftovers, and kids love it!

Serves 4 to 6

1 tablespoon extra-virgin olive oil

1 medium yellow onion, diced

1 red bell pepper, seeded and diced

1 pound ground turkey, chicken, or grass-fed beef

2½ tablespoons chili powder

1 tablespoon ground cumin

2 teaspoons fine sea salt

1 teaspoon oregano

1 teaspoon garlic powder

¼ teaspoon cayenne pepper

¾ cup chicken broth, homemade (page 243) or store-bought

1 (15-ounce) can red kidney beans, rinsed and drained

1 (15-ounce) can black beans, rinsed and drained

2 (15-ounce) cans pinto beans, rinsed and drained

2 (15-ounce) cans tomato sauce

1 (4-ounce) can green chiles

1 Preheat an electric pressure cooker using the **SAUTÉ** function.

2 When the display panel reads **HOT**, add the olive oil, onion, and bell pepper. Cook, stirring occasionally, until the onion is translucent, about 5 minutes. Add the turkey, chili powder, cumin, salt, oregano, garlic powder, and cayenne. Cook, stirring occasionally, until the turkey crumbles and is cooked through, 5 to 7 minutes.

3 Add the broth, beans, tomato sauce, and green chiles. Do *not* stir.

4 Place the lid on the cooker and make sure the vent valve is in the **SEALING** position. Select the **MANUAL/ PRESSURE COOK** function and **HIGH PRESSURE**. Use the +/- buttons until the display reads 10 minutes.

5 When the cooker beeps, let it naturally release the pressure until the display reads **LO:05**. Switch the vent valve from the **SEALING** to the **VENTING** position. Use caution while the steam escapes.

6 Serve warm.

Turkey Parm Meatloaf Minis

You're going to fall in love with these adorable meatloaf minis! Not only are they incredibly easy to throw together, but they are so darn tasty! Optionally, you can serve them with a piece of toasted sourdough or over your favorite pasta or zucchini noodles. They also pair fabulously with a Classic Caesar Salad (page 103).

Serves 4

1 pound ground turkey

1 large egg

¼ cup dried minced onion

2 tablespoons almond flour

1 tablespoon Italian seasoning, homemade (page 238) or store-bought

1 teaspoon garlic powder

1 teaspoon fine sea salt

½ teaspoon ground black pepper

½ cup chicken broth, homemade (page 243) or store-bought

1½ cups marinara sauce

2 slices mozzarella cheese (optional)

8 basil leaves, torn

1   In a large bowl, combine the turkey, egg, minced onion, almond flour, Italian seasoning, garlic powder, salt, and pepper. Mix well with your hands and divide into 4 equal portions. Shape each portion into an oval mound.

2   Add the broth and marinara to an electric pressure cooker. Place the mini meatloaves on top of the sauce.

3   Place the lid on the pressure cooker and make sure the vent valve is in the **SEALING** position. Select the **MANUAL/PRESSURE COOK** function and **HIGH PRESSURE**. Use the +/- buttons until the display reads 8 minutes.

4   When the cooker beeps, let it naturally release the pressure until the display reads **LO:05**. Switch the vent valve from the **SEALING** to the **VENTING** position. Use caution while the steam escapes.

5   Top each meatloaf with ½ slice mozzarella cheese (if using) and some torn basil. Place the lid back on the pressure cooker for 5 minutes to allow the cheese to melt. Serve warm.

Philly Steak Stir-Fry

This delicious, low-carb comfort bowl is reminiscent of a very high-carb favorite. If you are not a fan of cauliflower rice, I recommend quinoa or brown rice, or serve it as a sandwich. Simply toast your favorite bread or roll. Using a slotted spoon, place the filling on the bread, top with cheese, and broil until the cheese has melted, 1 to 2 minutes. Ladle some of the sauce into a ramekin and serve alongside the sandwich for dipping. This recipe is one that will please everyone!

Serves 4

1½ pounds rib eye steak, excess fat trimmed, thinly sliced

1 teaspoon fine sea salt

½ teaspoon ground black pepper

½ teaspoon garlic powder

2 tablespoons extra-virgin olive oil

1 pound cremini or button mushrooms, coarsely chopped

1 large green bell pepper, seeded and thinly sliced

1 medium yellow onion, thinly sliced

1 cup beef broth, homemade (page 243) or store-bought

2 tablespoons arrowroot powder

2 tablespoons cold water

4 cups cauliflower rice

4 slices provolone cheese (optional)

1   In a large bowl, toss the steak with the salt, pepper, and garlic powder.

2   Preheat an electric pressure cooker using the **SAUTÉ** function. When the display panel reads **HOT**, add the olive oil, mushrooms, bell pepper, and onion. Cook, stirring occasionally, for about 6 minutes. Add the steak and broth.

3   Place the lid on the cooker and make sure the vent valve is in the **SEALING** position. Select the **MANUAL/ PRESSURE COOK** function and **HIGH PRESSURE**. Use the +/- buttons until the display reads 3 minutes.

4   When the cooker beeps, switch the vent valve from the **SEALING** to the **VENTING** position. Use caution while the steam escapes.

5   Press the **CANCEL** button and then select the **SAUTÉ** function. In a small bowl, whisk the arrowroot powder into the cold water and add to the cooker, stirring until the sauce thickens, about 2 minutes.

6   Serve over the cauliflower rice, topped with provolone cheese, if desired.

Deconstructed Pork Souvlaki with Tzatziki Sauce

Souvlaki is a classic Greek dish, traditionally served on skewers. If you have a little extra time, I highly recommend skewering the pork, peppers, and onions instead and grilling them! It's absolutely perfect paired with Rice Pilaf (page 108) and a Greek salad or pita bread and Greek Potatoes (page 117)! If you do not consume pork, you can substitute chicken breasts or thighs.

Serves 4

FOR THE PORK

1½ pounds pork tenderloin, cut into 1-inch cubes

3 tablespoons extra-virgin olive oil

¼ cup fresh lemon juice

4 cloves garlic, minced

2 teaspoons fine sea salt

1 teaspoon ground black pepper

1½ teaspoons dried oregano

1 large green bell pepper, seeded and cut into 1-inch pieces

1 large yellow onion, cut into 1-inch pieces

2 tablespoons arrowroot powder

2 tablespoons cold water

FOR THE TZATZIKI SAUCE

1 cup shredded seeded cucumber

1 cup sour cream

1 teaspoon grated lemon zest

1 tablespoon fresh lemon juice

1 tablespoon dried dillweed

½ teaspoon garlic powder

½ teaspoon fine sea salt

¼ teaspoon ground black pepper

1   In a large bowl, combine the pork, olive oil, lemon juice, garlic, salt, pepper, and oregano. Stir until the pork is thoroughly seasoned. Allow the pork to marinate for 15 to 30 minutes.

2   Meanwhile, in a medium bowl, combine all of the tzatziki sauce ingredients and mix well. Cover and refrigerate until ready to serve.

3   Transfer the marinated pork to an electric pressure cooker, along with the bell pepper and onion.

4   Place the lid on the cooker and make sure the vent valve is in the **SEALING** position. Select the **MANUAL/ PRESSURE COOK** function and **HIGH PRESSURE**. Use the +/- buttons until the display reads 8 minutes.

5   When the cooker beeps, let it naturally release the pressure until the display reads **LO:05**. Switch the vent valve from the **SEALING** to the **VENTING** position. Use caution while the steam escapes.

6   Press the **CANCEL** button and then select the **SAUTÉ** function. In a small bowl, whisk the arrowroot powder into the cold water and add to the cooker, stirring until the sauce thickens, about 2 minutes.

7   Serve the pork with the tzatziki sauce.

Szechuan Honey Chicken Legs

This classic dish originates from the Sichuan province in China. Typically it is a very spicy dish, but this recipe tames it a bit with the honey. Try to find a chili garlic oil that has Szechuan peppercorns. If you can't, any chili oil will do.

Serves 4

8 chicken drumsticks, skin removed

1 teaspoon fine sea salt

½ teaspoon ground black pepper

¼ cup rice wine vinegar

¼ cup raw honey

1 tablespoon chili garlic oil

1½ teaspoons grated fresh ginger

⅓ cup coconut aminos or low-sodium soy sauce

1 cup plus 2 tablespoons cold water

2 tablespoons arrowroot powder

3 green onions, thinly sliced

1 pound frozen broccoli florets

2 to 4 cups cooked rice of choice (see page 22)

1   In an electric pressure cooker, combine the chicken, salt, pepper, vinegar, honey, chili garlic oil, ginger, coconut aminos, and 1 cup of the water.

2   Place the lid on the cooker and make sure the vent valve is in the **SEALING** position. Select the **MANUAL/PRESSURE COOK** function and **HIGH PRESSURE**. Use the +/- buttons until the display reads 20 minutes.

3   When the cooker beeps, let it naturally release the pressure until the display reads **LO:05**. Switch the vent valve from the **SEALING** to the **VENTING** position. Use caution while the steam escapes.

4   Press the **CANCEL** button and then select the **SAUTÉ** function. Transfer the chicken to a serving dish.

5   In a small bowl, whisk the arrowroot powder into the remaining 2 tablespoons cold water and add to the cooker. Add the green onions and broccoli and stir until the sauce thickens and the broccoli is crisp-tender, 6 to 8 minutes.

6   Pour the broccoli sauce over the chicken and serve over the rice.

5-Ingredient Meals

Penne Pasta Marinara... 170

Air-Fryer Mini
    Pepperoni Pizza........171

Curry Chicken Stir-Fry...172

One-Pot Air-Fryer
    Salmon and Potatoes ...174

Taco Chicken...........176

Buffalo Chicken Wraps ...176

Gluten-Free Chicken
    Strips................177

Classic Tuna Melts......179

Penne Pasta Marinara

This is such a simple pasta for any time of year! I like Jovial brand brown rice pasta and Rao's marinara sauce. I use bone broth for an extra boost of protein and collagen that you normally don't get from pasta, but you can use water. Homemade bone broth is the most budget-friendly option, but Kettle and Fire is a fantastic brand. Serve it with The Easiest Steamed Broccoli (page 110) for an extra boost of green!

Serves 2 to 3

8 ounces gluten-free penne

1 cup marinara sauce

1 cup chicken or beef broth, homemade (page 243) or store-bought

½ teaspoon fine sea salt

¼ teaspoon ground black pepper

1 In an electric pressure cooker, combine all of the ingredients.

2 Place the lid on the pressure cooker and make sure the vent valve is in the **SEALING** position. Select the **MANUAL/PRESSURE COOK** function and **HIGH PRESSURE**. Use the +/- buttons until the display reads 6 minutes.

3 When the cooker beeps, switch the vent valve from the **SEALING** to the **VENTING** position. Use caution while the steam escapes.

4 Serve warm.

Air-Fryer Mini Pepperoni Pizza

I love this delicious hack for making pizza with an almond flour tortilla instead
of a traditional dough crust. Siete makes delicious almond flour tortillas that work great
in a pinch when you don't have time to make your own. I find them in the freezer section
at Walmart or the refrigerated section at Costco. I like to use Rao's marinara—it's the best
tasting—and freshly grated Parmesan cheese. You can also use mozzarella. If you are
dairy-free, Violife makes an awesome plant-based cheese.

Serves 1

1 almond flour tortilla

Avocado cooking oil spray

2 tablespoons marinara

2 tablespoons shredded cheese
   of choice

6 nitrate-free pepperonis

1 Spray the tortilla with avocado oil cooking spray
and place it in the basket of a 5.3-quart air fryer. Place
the stainless steel trivet that came with your electric
pressure cooker on top of the tortilla to hold it in place
so that it doesn't blow around.

2 Air-fry for 3 minutes at 370°F. Remove the basket
from the air fryer housing and use an oven mitt to lift
the trivet off the tortilla. Flip the tortilla over and layer
the marinara, cheese, and pepperonis on top. Place the
trivet back on top of the mini pizza and place the basket
in the air fryer.

3 Air-fry for an additional 5 to 7 minutes at 370°F.
Use a pizza cutter to slice and serve warm.

Curry Chicken Stir-Fry

This Thai-inspired meal is one of my ever-faithful weeknight dinners. My family has been using this recipe for years. If you want to really kick up that umami flavor, add ½ sliced yellow onion and 1 tablespoon fish sauce. I use Native Forest coconut milk, Thai Kitchen curry paste, and Trader Joe's coconut aminos. I eat it as is but serve it over rice (see page 22) for my kiddos.

Serves 4

1 pound boneless, skinless chicken breasts

1 (13.5-ounce) can full-fat coconut milk

1 (4-ounce) jar red curry paste

2 tablespoons coconut aminos or low-sodium soy sauce

1 teaspoon fine sea salt

½ teaspoon ground black pepper

6 cups frozen stir-fry vegetable blend

1   In an electric pressure cooker, combine all of the ingredients.

2   Place the lid on the pressure cooker and make sure the vent valve is in the **SEALING** position. Select the **MANUAL/PRESSURE COOK** function and **HIGH PRESSURE**. Use the +/- buttons until the display reads 30 minutes.

3   When the cooker beeps, let it naturally release the pressure until the display reads **LO:05**. Switch the vent valve from the **SEALING** to the **VENTING** position. Use caution while the steam escapes.

4   Remove the chicken from the cooker and cut into thin slices. Return it to the pressure cooker and stir to combine. Serve warm.

One-Pot Air-Fryer Salmon and Potatoes

This one-pot salmon cooks up in under 30 minutes and is as simple as can be! It pairs nicely with a bagged salad mix or frozen broccoli coated in oil, salt, and pepper and tossed into the air fryer with the salmon for a green veggie on the side!

Serves 4

2 pounds baby gold potatoes, sweet potatoes, or red potatoes, cut into bite-size pieces

3 tablespoons extra-virgin olive oil

¾ teaspoon fine sea salt

½ teaspoon ground black pepper

1½ teaspoons chili lime seasoning

2 skin-on salmon fillets, pin bones removed

Fresh lemon slices, for serving (optional)

1 In a medium bowl, toss the potatoes with 2 tablespoons of the oil and the salt and pepper. Transfer to the basket of a 5.3-quart air fryer and cook at 375°F for 20 minutes, tossing halfway through.

2 While the potatoes cook, combine the chili lime seasoning with the remaining 1 tablespoon olive oil. Rub the mixture all over the salmon. Let sit to marinate.

3 Once the potatoes have finished cooking, place the salmon on top of the potatoes, skin side up, and cook for an additional 5 to 8 minutes, depending on the thickness of your salmon.

4 Divide the potatoes onto 4 plates, cut the salmon fillets in half, and serve warm with a spritz of lemon, if you like.

Taco Chicken

I'll bet that you probably have all of the ingredients on hand for this recipe right now! That's why it's one of my favorites. On top of that, it's an easy, one-pot pressure cooker meal, which makes it ideal for those busy weeknight dinners. I like to eat my taco chicken over a bed of lettuce, topped with fresh cilantro, avocado, lime juice, cheese, and homemade ranch.

Serves 4

1½ pounds boneless, skinless chicken breasts

1 (16-ounce) jar salsa

1 (16-ounce) bag frozen corn

1 (15-ounce) can black beans, rinsed and drained

¼ cup taco seasoning, homemade (page 234) or store-bought

1 In an electric pressure cooker, combine all of the ingredients.

2 Place the lid on the pressure cooker and make sure the vent valve is in the **SEALING** position. Select the **MANUAL/PRESSURE COOK** function and **HIGH PRESSURE**. Use the +/- buttons until the display reads 30 minutes.

3 When the cooker beeps, let it naturally release the pressure until the display reads **LO:05**. Switch the vent valve from the **SEALING** to the **VENTING** position. Use caution while the steam escapes.

4 Remove the chicken from the cooker and cut into thin slices. Return it to the pressure cooker and stir to combine. Serve warm.

Buffalo Chicken Wraps

This is one of our favorite easy lunches! If you don't want to make your own chicken strips, I like gluten-free Applegate strips. For this recipe, I use Siete almond flour tortillas.

Serves 4

8 almond flour tortillas or other tortillas of choice, warmed

1 recipe Strip Sauce (page 177)

1 cup coleslaw mix

1 recipe Gluten-Free Chicken Strips (page 177)

2 Roma tomatoes, sliced

Layer each tortilla with some strip sauce, coleslaw mix, chicken strips, and tomatoes. Drizzle with additional strip sauce.

Gluten-Free Chicken Strips

Who says you can't continue to eat your old favorites while losing weight? I was my mom's pickiest eater. I grew up on chicken fingers, french fries, and mac and cheese—all drowned in copious amounts of ketchup! You'd think with all the chicken strips I've consumed throughout my life that my love for them would wane, but not so. I'm a strip lover for life—although I have halfway outgrown my ketchup obsession.

Serves 4

1 pound boneless, skinless chicken breast tenders

1 large egg, beaten

1 tablespoon extra-virgin olive oil, plus more for air-frying

1 teaspoon garlic powder

1 teaspoon onion powder

1 teaspoon fine sea salt

½ teaspoon ground black pepper

½ cup gluten-free panko bread crumbs

1 recipe Strip Sauce (recipe follows), for serving

1 In a medium bowl, toss the chicken with the egg, oil, garlic powder, onion powder, salt, and pepper.

2 Put the crumbs in a wide, shallow bowl. Coat each strip of chicken in the bread crumbs, then place in a single layer in the basket of a 5.3-quart air fryer.

3 Lightly drizzle the strips with olive oil and air-fry at 360°F for 12 minutes, flipping the chicken over halfway through and giving each strip another light drizzle of oil.

4 Serve with the sauce.

Strip Sauce

This is one of our favorite sauces in the world, so we always keep it on hand. We use it as a dip for sweet potato fries, chicken strips, burgers, and wings or as a dressing for Buffalo chicken salad or wraps. It's as simple as it gets and really packs a lot of flavor into a dish!

Makes 1 cup

½ cup mayonnaise, homemade (page 240) or store-bought

½ cup Frank's RedHot sauce

Combine the mayo and hot sauce in a small bowl and stir until combined. Store in an airtight container in the refrigerator for up to 1 week.

Classic Tuna Melts

This recipe takes me straight back to childhood. It was always a special thing when my mom made tuna melts! You can dress them up by adding things like chopped celery or red onion and fresh herbs, or keep it simple as I do here. I use Dave's Killer Bread or homemade sourdough for this recipe. I recommend Woodstock organic sweet relish.

Serves 4

2 (5-ounce) cans wild-caught tuna, drained

½ cup mayonnaise, homemade (page 240) or store-bought, plus a little more for spreading

⅓ cup sweet relish

½ teaspoon fine sea salt

¼ teaspoon ground black pepper

8 slices bread of choice

4 slices cheddar cheese

1 In a large bowl, flake the tuna and mix in the mayo, relish, salt, and pepper.

2 Spread mayo on one side of each slice of bread and place them mayo side down. Top 4 slices with the tuna and cheese, and place the remaining 4 bread slices on top, mayo side up.

3 Place one sandwich in the basket of a 5.3-quart air fryer and air-fry at 360°F for 5 to 10 minutes, or until the cheese melts, flipping halfway through.

4 Repeat to cook the remaining sandwiches. Serve warm.

15-Minute Meals

Chicken Enchilada
   Roll-Ups 182

Deconstructed Stuffed
   Pepper Bowls 183

Mussels in Coconut-
   Lime Curry Sauce 184

Tuna Pasta Salad 186

Pick-Up Garlicky Herb
   Shrimp with Creamy
   Cocktail Sauce 189

Broccoli Chicken
   Alfredo 191

Easy Chicken Ramen 193

Swedish Meatballs 195

Egg Roll in a Bowl with
   Sriracha Mayo 196

Chicken Enchilada Roll-Ups

This is such an easy, versatile recipe because it can be served as a dip with chips, in a lettuce cup, or wrapped inside your favorite tortilla (I like Siete almond flour tortillas). Dress these up with cheese and sauce or dress them down by leaving the chicken mixture in a bowl and using it as a quick source of protein over salads throughout the week. This will become a go-to.

Serves 2 to 4

1 rotisserie chicken, skin and bones removed, meat shredded

½ cup Greek yogurt or dairy-free yogurt of choice

½ cup enchilada sauce

2 bell peppers (any color), seeded and finely chopped

1 (4-ounce) can diced green chiles

2 tablespoons taco seasoning, homemade (page 234) or store-bought

1 tablespoon fresh lime juice

½ teaspoon fine sea salt

Small tortillas of choice, warmed

1 head butterleaf lettuce

1   In a large bowl, combine the chicken, yogurt, enchilada sauce, bell peppers, green chiles, taco seasoning, lime juice, and salt. Stir to combine.

2   On each tortilla, place a lettuce leaf and a spoonful or two of the chicken mixture, then roll it up. Serve immediately.

Deconstructed Stuffed Pepper Bowls

I love a good stuffed pepper, but it can't be denied that they're a bit of a pain to eat. This is a shortcut to get the same stuffed pepper taste that we all love without the additional steps. For added veggie power, layer the bottom of the bowl with any mixed greens that you have on hand. Leftovers work well in a burrito for lunch the next day.

Serves 4 to 6

2 large bell peppers (any color), seeded and diced

¼ yellow onion, diced

½ bunch cilantro, stems finely chopped, leaves reserved for garnish

1 teaspoon fine sea salt

1 cup quinoa, rinsed and drained

1½ cups chicken broth, homemade (page 243) or store-bought

1 (15-ounce) can black beans, rinsed and drained

1 cup frozen yellow corn

2 tablespoons taco seasoning, homemade (page 234) or store-bought

2 teaspoons ground cumin

2 teaspoons dried minced onion

1½ teaspoons garlic powder

½ cup ranch dressing, homemade (page 153) or store-bought

1   In an electric pressure cooker, combine all of the ingredients except the ranch dressing.

2   Place the lid on the pressure cooker and make sure the vent valve is in the **SEALING** position. Select the **MANUAL/PRESSURE COOK** function and **HIGH PRESSURE**. Use the +/- buttons until the display reads 10 minutes.

3   When the cooker beeps, let it naturally release the pressure until the display reads **LO:05**. Switch the vent valve from the **SEALING** to the **VENTING** position. Use caution while the steam escapes.

4   Serve topped with the reserved cilantro leaves and ranch dressing.

Mussels in Coconut-Lime Curry Sauce

This Thai-style dish is a delightfully simple weeknight meal that feels extravagant. It also makes an excellent appetizer without the pasta—serve in a bowl with crusty bread for dipping into the savory sauce. Do not use frozen mussels because the texture becomes mealy. I recommend Thai Kitchen red curry paste, which can be found at most grocery stores.

Serves 4

2 pounds fresh mussels

2 tablespoons extra-virgin olive oil

1 small white onion, finely chopped

3 cloves garlic, minced

2½ tablespoons red curry paste

1 (13.5-ounce) can full-fat coconut milk

½ cup chicken broth, homemade (page 243) or store-bought

½ teaspoon fine sea salt

Grated zest and juice of ½ lime

12 ounces gluten-free linguine, cooked according to package instructions and drained

1 Before cooking, make sure the mussel shells are firmly closed. If any are open even slightly, give them a tap and see if they shut. If they do not close, discard them.

2 Rinse the mussels under cold water and remove the beard (the hairy fibers usually at the bottom of the mussels).

3 Preheat an electric pressure cooker using the **SAUTÉ** function.

4 When the display panel reads **HOT**, add the olive oil and onion. Cook, stirring occasionally, until the onion is translucent, about 5 minutes. Stir in the garlic and cook for 1 minute.

5 Add the curry paste, coconut milk, broth, salt, and mussels and stir to combine.

6 Place the lid on the cooker and make sure the vent valve is in the **SEALING** position. Select the **MANUAL/ PRESSURE COOK** function and **HIGH PRESSURE**. Use the +/- buttons until the display reads 2 minutes for smaller mussels or 3 for larger.

7 When the cooker beeps, switch the vent valve from the **SEALING** to the **VENTING** position. Use caution while the steam escapes.

8 Stir in the lime zest and juice. Serve the mussels and broth over the pasta.

Tuna Pasta Salad

This is a great pasta salad to take to a potluck party or for a quick, filling lunch. It packs lots of flavor yet comes together so easily that it's one of my go-to's. I like Jovial brand pasta. It is gluten-free and you can't even tell the difference!

Serves 4 to 6

8 ounces gluten-free small pasta shells, cooked according to package instructions and drained

2 (4.5-ounce) cans wild-caught tuna, drained and flaked

¾ cup mayonnaise, homemade (page 240) or store-bought

1½ cups thawed frozen peas

½ cup chopped celery

⅓ cup finely chopped red onion

2 tablespoons chopped fresh chives

1 tablespoon dried dillweed

1 teaspoon fine sea salt

½ teaspoon ground black pepper

In a large bowl, combine all of the ingredients and toss to mix well.

Pick-Up Garlicky Herb Shrimp with Creamy Cocktail Sauce

This is a great little appetizer or a beautiful shrimp to put over the Classic Caesar Salad (page 103). If you're not a big salad lover, pair it with The Easiest Steamed Broccoli (page 110) and Garlic Mashed Cauliflower (page 113)!

Serves 4

1 pound large shrimp, peeled and deveined (tails left on)

¼ cup extra-virgin olive oil

2 cloves garlic, minced

½ teaspoon fine sea salt

½ teaspoon red pepper flakes

2 tablespoons fresh parsley, finely chopped

½ cup cocktail sauce

¼ cup mayonnaise, homemade (page 240) or store-bought

4 lemon wedges (optional)

1 In a large bowl, toss the shrimp with the oil, garlic, salt, pepper flakes, and parsley.

2 Preheat an electric pressure cooker using the **SAUTÉ** function. When the display panel reads **HOT**, add the shrimp and cook, stirring occasionally, for about 8 minutes, or until the shrimp is no longer opaque. (Alternatively, you can cook the shrimp in a large skillet over medium-high heat.)

3 Transfer the shrimp to a plate and let stand for 5 minutes. While the shrimp cools, mix the cocktail sauce and mayo together in a small bowl.

4 Serve the shrimp with the sauce and lemon wedges, if desired.

Broccoli Chicken Alfredo

Incredibly simple, this dairy-free chicken Alfredo will become an instant classic in your household! If you do not have a rotisserie chicken on hand, throw 2 or 3 chicken breasts in your pressure cooker with ½ cup water or broth, salt, and pepper. Cook at high pressure for 25 minutes, then shred and season with additional salt and pepper. You can also use frozen chicken breasts; just increase the cook time to 30 minutes. This meal never ceases to have everyone running back for more.

Serves 6

FOR THE SAUCE

2 cups water

1 cup raw cashews

2 tablespoons nutritional yeast

2 cloves garlic, peeled

2 teaspoons fine sea salt, plus more to taste

½ teaspoon ground black pepper, plus more to taste

FOR THE FETTUCINE, BROCCOLI, AND CHICKEN

1 pound gluten-free fettucine, cooked according to package instructions and drained

1 recipe The Easiest Steamed Broccoli (page 110)

1 rotisserie chicken, skin and bones discarded, meat shredded

1 Combine all of the sauce ingredients in a high-powered blender. Blend on high until the sauce begins to steam and thicken, about 8 minutes. (If you do not have a high-powered blender, you can blend using a regular blender and then warm the sauce in a saucepan over medium heat, whisking constantly, until it thickens.) Set aside.

2 In a large bowl, toss the fettucine, broccoli, and chicken with the sauce. Season with additional salt and pepper, if needed.

Easy Chicken Ramen

Who else grew up on Top Ramen? We would take uncooked packages to school, break up the ramen in the package, sprinkle it with that special seasoning packet and eat it raw! Good times. That is, until you discover that it's chock-full of artificial flavors and additives! I'm not a fan of restriction, but I am always in favor of substitution. So, I set out to create a delicious ramen—reminiscent of our childhoods but with functional whole food ingredients—that is as nourishing for the body as it is tantalizing for the taste buds!

If you're cooking for six people, you can add a third block of ramen without doubling any of the other ingredients. You can also use low-carb hearts of palm noodles in this recipe, but since they are precooked, don't stir them in until the end when you stir in the carrots.

Serves 4

1 tablespoon toasted sesame oil

1 tablespoon extra-virgin olive oil

1 pound boneless, skinless chicken breasts, cut into ½-inch pieces

1 teaspoon fine sea salt, plus more to taste

½ teaspoon ground black pepper, plus more to taste

2 blocks brown rice ramen noodles

4 green onions, thinly sliced

3 tablespoons red curry paste

2 tablespoons coconut aminos or low-sodium soy sauce

2 teaspoons grated fresh ginger

5 cups chicken broth, homemade (page 243) or store-bought

1 tablespoon dried minced onion

2 teaspoons garlic powder

2 carrots, cut into ribbons

1 tablespoon sesame seeds (optional)

3 tablespoons fresh cilantro leaves (optional)

4 to 6 Soft-Boiled Eggs (recipe follows), peeled and cut in half

1 Preheat an electric pressure cooker using the **SAUTÉ** function.

2 When the display panel reads **HOT**, add the sesame oil, olive oil, chicken, salt, and pepper. Cook, stirring occasionally, until the chicken is almost cooked through, about 5 minutes.

3 Add the ramen noodles, green onions, red curry paste, coconut aminos, ginger, broth, minced onion, and garlic powder and stir to combine.

4 Place the lid on the cooker and make sure the vent valve is in the **SEALING** position. Select the **MANUAL/PRESSURE COOK** function and **HIGH PRESSURE**. Use the +/- buttons until the display reads 1 minute.

Recipe continues

5 When the cooker beeps, switch the vent valve from the **SEALING** to the **VENTING** position. Use caution while the steam escapes.

6 Stir in the carrot ribbons and serve topped with the sesame seeds and cilantro (if you like), plus the soft-boiled eggs. Season with salt and pepper.

Soft-Boiled Eggs

I love a good jammy egg. It's one of the most common things I have for breakfast. Delicious with sourdough toast, on an arugula salad, or paired with ramen. You can't really go wrong with a soft-boiled egg.

Makes 12 eggs

1 cup water
12 large eggs, or as many
   as desired

1 Pour the water into an electric pressure cooker and place the steamer basket or trivet on top. Place the eggs in the steamer basket.

2 Place the lid on the pressure cooker and make sure the vent valve is in the **SEALING** position. Select the **MANUAL/PRESSURE COOK** function and **LOW PRESSURE**. Use the +/- buttons until the display reads 3 minutes.

3 When the cooker beeps, switch the vent valve from the **SEALING** to the **VENTING** position. Use caution while the steam escapes.

4 Immediately place the eggs in an ice bath for 5 minutes to halt the cooking process. Store the eggs in the refrigerator for up to 6 days.

Swedish Meatballs

Swedish meatballs aren't actually Swedish. They're just a twist on a traditional meatball served with a gravy-style sauce! These are delicious served over Garlic Mashed Cauliflower (page 113) with a side of The Easiest Steamed Broccoli (page 110).

Serves 4

1 pound grass-fed ground beef

1 large egg

¼ cup gluten-free seasoned bread crumbs

2 tablespoons dried minced onion

½ teaspoon garlic powder

⅛ teaspoon ground nutmeg

1 teaspoon fine sea salt

½ teaspoon ground black pepper

1 tablespoon extra-virgin olive oil

2 cups beef broth, homemade (page 243) or store-bought

1 cup canned full-fat coconut milk

1 tablespoon Dijon mustard

1 tablespoon Worcestershire sauce

3 tablespoons arrowroot powder

3 tablespoons cold water

2 tablespoons fresh parsley (optional)

1 Preheat an electric pressure cooker using the **SAUTÉ** function.

2 In a large bowl, combine the ground beef, egg, bread crumbs, minced onion, garlic powder, nutmeg, salt, and pepper. Mix together with your hands, then divide into 16 equal balls.

3 When the display panel reads **HOT**, add the oil and the meatballs to the pot. Allow the meatballs to brown on all sides, turning occasionally, for about 5 minutes. Add the broth, coconut milk, Dijon, and Worcestershire sauce.

4 Place the lid on the cooker and make sure the vent valve is in the **SEALING** position. Select the **MANUAL/PRESSURE COOK** function, **HIGH PRESSURE**, and use the +/- buttons until the display reads 4 minutes.

5 When the cooker beeps, let it naturally release the pressure until the display reads **LO:02**. Switch the vent valve from the **SEALING** to the **VENTING** position. Use caution while the steam escapes.

6 Using a slotted spoon, transfer the meatballs to a serving bowl.

7 Press the **CANCEL** button and then select the **SAUTÉ** function. In a small bowl, whisk the arrowroot powder into the cold water and add to the cooker, stirring until the sauce thickens, about 2 minutes. Pour the sauce over the meatballs and garnish with the parsley, if desired.

Egg Roll in a Bowl with Sriracha Mayo

Here's a new spin on the classic Chinese take-out dish: all of the delicious, good-for-you fresh flavors of an egg roll made with whole food ingredients and none of the deep-fried drawbacks! This recipe can also be made on the stovetop. Instead of pressure cooking, simply cook the vegetables down on the stovetop for 8 to 10 additional minutes.

Serves 4

FOR THE EGG ROLL BOWL

1 teaspoon toasted sesame oil

½ medium white onion, thinly sliced

4 cloves garlic, minced

1½ pounds ground pork or chicken

1 (16-ounce) bag coleslaw mix

½ cup shredded carrot

½ cup shredded red cabbage

⅓ cup coconut aminos or low-sodium soy sauce

1 teaspoon rice vinegar

½ teaspoon onion powder

¼ teaspoon ground ginger

2 green onions, thinly sliced

FOR THE SRIRACHA MAYO

½ cup mayonnaise, homemade (page 240) or store-bought

2 tablespoons sriracha

1½ teaspoons coconut aminos or low-sodium soy sauce

½ teaspoon garlic powder

¼ teaspoon fine sea salt

⅛ teaspoon ground black pepper

1 Preheat an electric pressure cooker using the **SAUTÉ** function.

2 When the display panel reads **HOT**, add the oil, onion, and garlic. Cook, stirring occasionally, for 3 minutes. Add the ground pork and cook, stirring occasionally and breaking it up with a spatula, until browned, about 5 minutes. Add the coleslaw, carrot, red cabbage, coconut aminos, vinegar, onion powder, and ginger.

3 Place the lid on the cooker and make sure the vent valve is in the **SEALING** position. Select the **MANUAL/PRESSURE COOK** function, **HIGH PRESSURE**, and use the +/- buttons until the display reads 2 minutes.

4 Meanwhile, in a small bowl, stir together all of the sriracha mayo ingredients.

5 When the cooker beeps, switch the vent valve from the **SEALING** to the **VENTING** position. Use caution while the steam escapes.

6 Serve warm, topped with the green onions and drizzled with the sriracha mayo.

Casseroles, Sheet Pans, and Skillets

Green Chile Chicken
　　Enchiladas 200

Easy Egg Bite
　　Casserole 201

Cauliflower Tinga
　　Tacos 202

Spaghetti Squash
　　Lasagna Casserole 203

Simple Chicken Sausage
　　Sheet Pan 205

Oven-Baked Chicken
　　Schnitzel with Fries . . . 206

Sheet Pan Fajitas 208

Beefy Enchilada
　　Skillet 210

Hamburger Tacos 213

Green Chile Chicken Enchiladas

Have a friend who just had a baby? Want to bulk up your freezer meal stash? This is a great make-now-and-eat-later dish! Simply put it all together and store in the freezer until you're ready to bake. If you're cooking for a crowd, I recommend doubling this recipe and baking it in a 9 × 13-inch glass dish.

Violife cheese is a great plant-based option if you're dairy-free. If you do not have a rotisserie chicken handy, you can use 1½ pounds cooked chicken breast.

Serves 6

Cooking oil spray

½ rotisserie chicken, skin and bones discarded, meat shredded

1 cup plain Greek yogurt or dairy-free yogurt of choice

1 (15-ounce) jar green enchilada sauce

2 tablespoons taco seasoning, homemade (page 234) or store-bought

7 or 8 corn tortillas, torn into 2- to 3-inch pieces

6 ounces shredded mozzarella cheese

1 Preheat the oven to 350°F. Spray an 8 × 8-inch glass baking dish with cooking oil spray.

2 In a large bowl, combine the chicken, yogurt, ¼ cup of the enchilada sauce, and the taco seasoning and mix well.

3 Spread about one-quarter of the remaining enchilada sauce in the bottom of the prepared baking dish, then lay about one-quarter of the tortilla pieces in a single layer over the sauce. Spread about one-quarter of the chicken mixture over the tortillas, then top with about one-quarter of the cheese. Repeat to make three more layers.

4 Cover the baking dish with aluminum foil and bake for 30 minutes. Remove the foil and turn on the broiler. Broil for 3 to 5 minutes, or until the cheese begins to brown. Let sit for 5 minutes before serving.

Easy Egg Bite Casserole

I love egg bites, but I don't love cleaning egg out of my muffin pan. This easy egg bite casserole is much easier to make and clean up, saving you time twice over!

Serves 6

Cooking oil spray

12 large eggs

1½ cups cottage cheese

1 teaspoon fine sea salt

½ teaspoon ground black pepper

6 strips nitrate-free bacon, cooked and crumbled

1 cup baby spinach, chopped

½ large red bell pepper, seeded and chopped

1 Preheat the oven to 350°F. Spray an 8 × 8-inch baking pan with cooking oil spray.

2 Blend the eggs, cottage cheese, salt, and pepper in a high-powered blender for 30 seconds.

3 Layer the crumbled bacon, spinach, and bell pepper in the prepared baking pan. Pour the egg mixture over the top.

4 Bake for 40 minutes, or until the middle firms up and has just a little bit of jiggle to it. Let cool for 5 minutes before cutting and serving.

Cauliflower Tinga Tacos

Zesty! Spicy! And so dangerously good! These vegetarian tacos will be a dinnertime smash hit. If you aren't a fan of heat, you can mellow the spiciness of the chipotle peppers with sour cream. And if you really like it hot, you won't need the sour cream at all. I usually use homemade corn or flour tortillas. If you don't want to make your own, I like Siete almond flour tortillas or Food for Life sprouted corn tortillas.

   If you do not have an air fryer, you can spread out the cauliflower-chickpea mixture on a rimmed baking sheet and bake in the oven at 400°F for 30 minutes.

Serves 4

FOR THE CAULIFLOWER TINGA

1 small head cauliflower, cored and cut into small florets

1 (15-ounce) can chickpeas, rinsed and drained

1 tablespoon extra-virgin olive oil

1 teaspoon fine sea salt

1 teaspoon ground black pepper

½ red onion

4 cloves garlic, peeled

1 (3-ounce) can chipotle peppers in adobo

1 teaspoon 100% pure maple syrup

1 teaspoon dried oregano

FOR THE TACOS

8 tortillas

¼ cup sour cream or Greek yogurt

½ cup shredded red cabbage

1 large avocado, pitted, peeled, and sliced

½ cup chopped fresh cilantro leaves

2 limes, cut into wedges

1 Combine the cauliflower, chickpeas, olive oil, salt, pepper, red onion, and garlic cloves in the basket of a 5.3-quart air fryer and toss to mix. Air-fry at 380°F for 15 minutes.

2 Transfer the red onion and garlic cloves to a high-powered blender and add the chipotle peppers in adobo, maple syrup, and oregano. Blend until smooth.

3 Transfer the cauliflower and chickpeas to a large bowl, add the blended chipotle sauce, and toss to mix.

4 Fill each tortilla with some of the cauliflower mixture and top with sour cream, red cabbage, avocado, cilantro, and lime juice. Serve warm.

Spaghetti Squash Lasagna Casserole

Have leftover spaghetti squash? Try this recipe! It bakes up nicely and isn't watery like vegetable-based lasagnas often are. I always add a bit of green to our dinner plate as well, like a side of green beans. Just pop your green beans in the pressure cooker with ¾ cup water or broth, salt, pepper, garlic powder, and dried minced onion and cook for 3 minutes at high pressure. So easy and so tasty! My favorite marinara sauces are Otamot spicy organic, Sonoma Gourmet organic roasted garlic, and Rao's.

Serves 6 to 8

1 cup water

1 small to medium spaghetti squash

3 tablespoons extra-virgin olive oil, plus more for greasing

¾ teaspoon fine sea salt

½ teaspoon ground black pepper

Juice of 2 lemons

1 (10-ounce) package firm tofu, drained and pressed for 15 minutes

5 tablespoons nutritional yeast

½ cup packed fresh basil

1 tablespoon dried oregano

¼ cup freshly grated Parmesan cheese

1 (16-ounce) jar marinara sauce

3 kale leaves, stemmed and chopped

1 Preheat the oven to 375°F.

2 Pour the water into an electric pressure cooker, place the trivet inside, and then place the spaghetti squash on the trivet.

3 Place the lid on the pressure cooker and make sure the vent valve is in the **SEALING** position. Select the **MANUAL/PRESSURE COOK** function and **HIGH PRESSURE**. Use the **+/-** buttons until the display reads 15 minutes.

4 When the cooker beeps, switch the vent valve from the **SEALING** to the **VENTING** position. Use caution while the steam escapes.

5 While the squash cooks, combine the olive oil, salt, pepper, lemon juice, tofu, nutritional yeast, basil, oregano, and Parmesan cheese in a high-powered blender and blend until it reaches a ricotta-like consistency, or smooth, if preferred.

6 Cut the squash in half lengthwise and remove the seeds. Shred the flesh with a fork.

7 Grease a 9 × 13-inch glass baking dish lightly with olive oil. Spread half of the spaghetti squash in the bottom of the dish, then top with half of the tofu

Recipe continues

mixture and smooth with a spoon. Add half of the marinara and smooth flat, then sprinkle with half of the kale. Repeat to make another layer on top.

8 Cover the dish with aluminum foil and bake for 20 minutes. Remove the foil and bake for an additional 10 minutes. Let cool for 10 minutes before serving.

Simple Chicken Sausage Sheet Pan

This simple sheet pan dinner is so packed full of flavor, it's going to surprise you. The leftovers are delicious for a savory breakfast in the a.m. with a fried egg on top. I love Aidells chicken and apple sausage, or you can try Teton Waters Ranch grass-fed beef sausage or your sausage of choice, as long as it is already cooked or smoked (not raw).

Serves 6

8 medium red potatoes, cut into 1-inch cubes

4 (3-ounce) fully cooked chicken sausages, cut into ½-inch pieces

12 ounces fresh or frozen broccoli florets

½ cup extra-virgin olive oil

¼ cup coconut aminos or low-sodium soy sauce

2 tablespoons Dijon mustard

1 tablespoon Frank's RedHot sauce

4 cloves garlic, minced

1 teaspoon onion powder

1 teaspoon fine sea salt

½ teaspoon red pepper flakes

½ cup ranch dressing, homemade (page 153) or store-bought (optional)

1 Preheat the oven to 425°F. Line a rimmed baking sheet with parchment paper.

2 Put the potatoes in a medium bowl. In a large bowl, combine the sausage and broccoli.

3 In a small bowl, whisk together the olive oil, coconut aminos, Dijon, hot sauce, garlic, onion powder, sea salt, and red pepper flakes.

4 Pour half of the sauce over the potatoes and the other half over the sausage and broccoli. Mix separately until each is thoroughly coated in the sauce.

5 Transfer the potatoes to the prepared baking sheet and bake for 15 minutes. Push the potatoes to one half of the sheet and add the sausage and broccoli in a single layer on the other half. Bake for 20 minutes.

6 Serve warm with ranch dressing, if desired.

Oven-Baked Chicken Schnitzel with Fries

This dinner is an absolute winner! It combines breaded chicken and fries, two of everyone's favorite things, but in a lighter, healthier way. I like to serve this meal with a bagged salad mix. The Taylor Farms organic Mediterranean Crunch chopped salad kit from Costco is a family favorite. Serve the chicken over the salad and the fries on the side. This will be a recipe you keep coming back to.

Serves 4

FOR THE FRIES

Olive oil spray

2 large russet potatoes

2 tablespoons extra-virgin olive oil

1½ teaspoons fine sea salt

FOR THE CHICKEN

2 large boneless, skinless chicken breasts

2 large eggs

1 cup almond flour

1 teaspoon garlic powder

1¼ teaspoons fine sea salt

½ teaspoon ground black pepper

Olive oil spray

1 lemon, cut into wedges (optional)

1   Preheat the oven to 400°F. Spray a dark rimmed baking sheet with olive oil spray.

2   Depending on the thickness of the potatoes, cut them lengthwise in halves or in thirds, and then into ¼-inch-thick fries. Soak the cut fries in a bowl of cold water for 15 to 30 minutes. Drain and pat dry. Return the fries to the bowl and toss with the olive oil and salt. Spread out the fries in a single layer on the prepared baking sheet and bake for 20 minutes.

3   Meanwhile, cut each chicken breast in half through its thickness so you end up with 4 thin cutlets. Using a meat mallet, gently pound each cutlet to about ¼ inch thick.

4   Beat the eggs in a medium bowl. In another medium bowl, combine the almond flour, garlic powder, salt, and pepper. Coat each piece of chicken in the egg mixture, then coat completely in the almond flour mixture.

5   When the fries have cooked for 20 minutes, flip them over and push them onto one half of the baking sheet. Place the breaded chicken pieces on the other half of the baking sheet and spray lightly with olive oil spray. Bake for 20 to 25 minutes, or until the fries are crispy and the tops of the chicken are lightly browned.

6   Serve warm with a spritz of lemon, if desired.

Sheet Pan Fajitas

The bulk of the time spent on this meal is all in preparation. I recommend chopping all of the veggies and chicken beforehand so it's ready for the oven when you're ready to cook. This can be served with your favorite salsa, pico de gallo, or hot sauce. I like to make my own taco seasoning, but you can buy Siete brand, which has no added sugars or fillers.

Serves 4

1 pound boneless, skinless chicken breasts, halved and cut into ¼-inch strips

1 red bell pepper, seeded and thinly sliced

1 yellow bell pepper, seeded and thinly sliced

1 green bell pepper, seeded and thinly sliced

1 jalapeño, thinly sliced

1 medium white onion, thinly sliced

1 tablespoon minced garlic

1 tablespoon extra-virgin olive oil

¼ cup taco seasoning, homemade (page 234) or store-bought

½ teaspoon fine sea salt

¼ teaspoon ground black pepper

8 corn tortillas, warmed

¼ cup plain Greek yogurt or dairy-free yogurt of choice

½ bunch cilantro, chopped (optional)

1 lime, cut into wedges

1 Preheat the oven to 375°F. Line a rimmed baking sheet with parchment paper.

2 In a large bowl, combine the chicken, bell peppers, jalapeño, onion, garlic, olive oil, taco seasoning, salt, and pepper and toss until everything is thoroughly coated. Transfer to the prepared baking sheet and spread out in a single layer.

3 Bake for 30 to 35 minutes, or until the chicken is fully cooked.

4 Divide the chicken, peppers, and onion between the tortillas. Top with the yogurt and cilantro (if using) and serve with a spritz of lime.

Beefy Enchilada Skillet

I love a good shortcut! Instead of spending time rolling tortillas or creating layers for a traditional enchilada casserole, this is a great way to enjoy some of your favorite flavors in a less labor-intensive way. I am a big fan of Truly Grass Fed cheeses, but you can use any cheese you like (or omit the cheese entirely). In addition, if you have fresh cilantro on hand, this would be a great place to use it! I know not everyone cares for the flavor, but if you love it as much as I do, about ½ cup chopped leaves, stirred into this dish at the end, with the cheese and tortillas, is divine!

Serves 4

1 tablespoon extra-virgin olive oil

½ medium yellow onion, diced

1 large red bell pepper, seeded and diced

2 cloves garlic, minced

1 pound grass-fed ground beef

2 cups chopped zucchini

1 (15-ounce can) black beans, rinsed and drained

1 (15-ounce) can tomato sauce

1 tablespoon chili powder

1 teaspoon ground cumin

½ teaspoon garlic powder

¼ teaspoon dried oregano

½ teaspoon fine sea salt

¼ teaspoon ground black pepper

½ cup shredded mild cheddar cheese

4 (6-inch) corn or flour tortillas, cut into ½-inch strips

¼ cup sliced green onions

1 avocado, pitted, peeled, and sliced

1 teaspoon red pepper flakes

1 Preheat a large cast-iron skillet over medium-high heat. Add the olive oil, onion, bell pepper, and garlic and cook, stirring occasionally, for 3 minutes. Add the ground beef and cook, stirring and breaking it up, until the meat is about three-quarters of the way cooked, about 5 minutes.

2 Stir in the zucchini, black beans, tomato sauce, chili powder, cumin, garlic powder, oregano, salt, and black pepper. Cook for about 3 minutes, stirring occasionally, until the bell pepper has softened.

3 Stir in ¼ cup of the cheese and the tortilla strips. Reduce the heat to medium-low, cover, and cook for 10 minutes.

4 Top with the remaining ¼ cup cheese and the green onions. Cover and cook until the cheese has melted, about 1 minute. Top with the sliced avocado and red pepper flakes and serve.

Hamburger Tacos

My aunt Kim says that her death row meal is a McDonald's french fries, an LDC (large Diet Coke), and a Big Mac. There's just something so incredibly satisfying about the meal that most of us grew up with. I don't believe in restriction, but I do believe in substitution, so I found a way to re-create an unhealthy classic with a good-for-you twist!

Serves 5

FOR THE SAUCE

¼ cup mayonnaise, homemade (page 240) or store-bought

1½ tablespoons sugar-free ketchup

1 tablespoon sweet relish

½ teaspoon apple cider vinegar

⅛ teaspoon fine sea salt (optional)

FOR THE TACOS

1 pound grass-fed ground beef

1¼ teaspoons fine sea salt

1 teaspoon onion powder

½ teaspoon ground black pepper

1 tablespoon avocado oil

5 almond flour tortillas or tortillas of choice

1 head romaine lettuce, cored and shredded

1 vine-ripened tomato, thinly sliced

1 In a small bowl, combine all of the sauce ingredients and mix well. Cover and refrigerate until ready to serve.

2 Heat a large cast-iron skillet over medium-high heat.

3 In a medium bowl, combine the ground beef, salt, onion powder, and pepper. Gently mix the ingredients together; do not overwork the meat or it can become tough. Divide the mixture into 5 equal portions. Roll each portion into a ball.

4 Add the avocado oil to the skillet. Once the oil is hot, add one ball of beef to the skillet and place a tortilla over the top. Press the tortilla down on the ball so that it flattens. Let cook for 3 minutes, then flip and cook it tortilla-side down for 3 minutes. Tilt the patty and tortilla to drain off the excess grease, then remove it from the pan and place it on a paper towel–lined plate. Cook the remaining patties and tortillas in the same fashion.

5 Smother each burger taco in the sauce and top with shredded lettuce and tomato.

Sweet Tooth

Mini Maple Vanilla
  Nut Cakes 217

Rice Pudding Sundae. . . . 218

Carrot Cake with Cashew
  Cream Frosting 220

Peanut Butter Chocolate
  Crispy Rice Treats 223

S'mores for Me Dip. 224

Make-Your-Own
  Mallows. 225

Caramel Chocolate
  Turtles 226

Ooey-Gooey Caramel. . . . 227

Dairy-Free Tres Leches. . 229

Tropical Fruit Skewers
  with Caramel Drizzle. . 231

Mini Maple Vanilla Nut Cakes

These little cakes are the perfect after-dinner delight! They are vegan and gluten-free and they freeze well for those moments when the sweet tooth won't stop knocking. If you do not have flax meal on hand and are not vegan, you can replace the flax meal and water with 6 large eggs.

Serves 6 to 12

Cooking oil spray

¾ cup water

6 tablespoons flax meal

1 cup coconut flour

1 teaspoon baking soda

½ teaspoon fine sea salt

¾ cup canned full-fat coconut milk

½ cup 100% pure maple syrup, plus more for drizzling

¼ cup extra-virgin olive oil

4 teaspoons pure vanilla extract

¼ cup chia seeds

¼ cup chopped walnuts

1 cup sliced strawberries

1 Preheat the oven to 350°F. Grease a 12-cup muffin pan with cooking oil spray.

2 In a medium bowl, combine the water and flax meal. Stir together and let sit for 8 minutes.

3 In a large bowl, combine the coconut flour, baking soda, and salt and stir. Add the coconut milk, maple syrup, olive oil, vanilla extract, chia seeds, and walnuts. Stir together until completely combined.

4 Add the flax mixture to the coconut mixture and stir. The mixture will be thick. Use a ¼-cup measuring cup to evenly distribute the batter into the prepared muffin cups. Gently press the mixture down so the cups are filled out and the tops are smooth.

5 Bake for 30 minutes, or until a toothpick inserted into the center of the cakes comes out clean.

6 Let cool for 5 minutes, then turn the pan over onto a cooling rack. Serve the cakes upside down, topped with strawberries and a drizzle of maple syrup.

Rice Pudding Sundae

When I was growing up, my mom always repurposed leftover rice with milk and cinnamon sugar for a delicious after-dinner dessert. This is a fun spin on a childhood staple for me. It's a treat for kids and adults alike!

Serves 4 to 6

FOR THE RICE PUDDING

2½ cups water

1 cup short-grain brown rice

FOR THE SAUCE

½ cup canned full-fat coconut milk

¼ cup 100% pure maple syrup

¼ cup unsweetened almond (or other) milk, homemade (page 234) or store-bought

1 large egg plus 1 large egg yolk

1 teaspoon pure vanilla extract

1 tablespoon ground cinnamon

¼ teaspoon ground nutmeg

¼ teaspoon fine sea salt

TOPPING SUGGESTIONS

Shredded coconut

Nuts and seeds

Sliced fresh fruit

Ooey-Gooey Caramel (page 227)

Chocolate sauce (page 57)

Dried fruit

Granola

Chocolate chips

1 In an electric pressure cooker, combine the water and rice.

2 Place the lid on the pressure cooker and make sure the vent valve is in the **SEALING** position. Select the **MANUAL/PRESSURE COOK** function and **HIGH PRESSURE**. Use the +/- buttons until the display reads 30 minutes.

3 Meanwhile, in a large bowl, whisk together the coconut milk, maple syrup, almond milk, whole egg and egg yolk, vanilla extract, cinnamon, nutmeg, and salt until smooth.

4 When the cooker beeps, let it naturally release the pressure until the display reads **LO:05**. Switch the vent valve from the **SEALING** to the **VENTING** position. Use caution while the steam escapes.

5 Stir in the sauce mixture. Select the **SAUTÉ** function and stir continuously for 6 minutes, or until the rice has thickened. Serve hot or store in an airtight container in the refrigerator until chilled. Serve with assorted toppings and sauces for a fun rice pudding sundae.

Carrot Cake with Cashew Cream Frosting

Carrot cake is my dad's favorite dessert. He has been focusing on cleaning up his diet this year after having a stroke. I made this for his last birthday and it was a hit! It's light but so rich that he didn't miss the gluten or ultra-refined sugars at all.

Serves 10 to 12

Cooking oil spray

2 large eggs

¼ cup ghee or grass-fed butter

¼ cup 100% pure maple syrup

¼ cup plus 2 tablespoons coconut sugar

⅔ cup unsweetened applesauce

1½ teaspoons baking soda

1 teaspoon aluminum-free baking powder

1 teaspoon ground cinnamon

½ teaspoon fine sea salt

⅔ cup unsweetened vanilla almond (or other) milk, homemade (page 234) or store-bought

1 cup tightly packed superfine blanched almond flour

1 cup old-fashioned rolled oats

1 cup grated carrots

½ cup chopped pecans or walnuts

1 recipe Cashew Cream Cheese Frosting (recipe follows)

1   Preheat the oven to 350°F. Coat a 9-inch round cake pan with cooking oil spray.

2   In a high-powered blender, combine the eggs, ghee, maple syrup, coconut sugar, applesauce, baking soda, baking powder, cinnamon, salt, almond milk, almond flour, and oats. Blend on high until smooth, about 1 minute. Stir in the grated carrots and ¼ cup of the chopped pecans, then pour the batter into the prepared cake pan.

3   Cover with aluminum foil and bake for 20 minutes. Remove the foil and bake for an additional 15 minutes, or until a toothpick inserted in the center comes out clean.

4   Let cool for 10 minutes, then transfer the cake to a serving platter. Let cool completely before frosting, then sprinkle the top with the remaining ¼ cup pecans.

Cashew Cream Cheese Frosting

I adore cream cheese frosting, especially spread on carrot cake—it's the only way to have it, IMO. But when I was pregnant with my fourth baby, I developed a severe allergic reaction to cream cheese. Always in favor of substitution instead of restriction, I found a better way to make it that doesn't require dairy at all! If you're a big fan of frosting, double this recipe for the Carrot Cake (page 220). If you like a lighter layer, one batch is sufficient.

Makes ⅔ cup

1 cup raw cashews, soaked for 4 hours and drained

¼ cup 100% pure maple syrup

2 tablespoons unsweetened vanilla almond (or other) milk, homemade (page 234) or store-bought

2 teaspoons pure vanilla extract

1 Combine all of the ingredients in a high-powered blender. Blend on high for 5 minutes, until smooth. As the blender mixture warms, the cashews will thicken.

2 Set aside to thicken and cool for about 5 minutes before using.

Peanut Butter Chocolate Crispy Rice Treats

The quality of these awesome little treats is all dependent on the chocolate, peanut butter, and puffed rice you choose. I like Enjoy Life chocolate chips because they are allergy-friendly and made with only three ingredients: unsweetened chocolate, cocoa butter, and cane sugar. I like Kirkland organic peanut butter because it's made with only peanuts; other peanut butters can be full of seed oils, emulsifiers, and sugars. And I like Nature's Path organic rice puffs cereal because it contains only puffed brown rice. Mainstream puffed rice cereal isn't actually whole rice at all and has added sugars and synthetic vitamins to try to make up for it. Don't be fooled.

Makes 18 treats

3 cups puffed rice cereal

¾ cup semisweet chocolate chips

2 heaping tablespoons peanut butter

1 Put the puffed rice cereal in a medium bowl.

2 In a small saucepan, melt the chocolate and peanut butter together over medium heat, stirring continuously.

3 Pour the melted mixture over the puffed rice cereal and stir to combine.

4 Spoon the mixture into 18 cups of a mini-muffin pan, or do it drop-biscuit style and spoon the mixture onto a rimmed baking sheet lined with parchment paper.

5 Refrigerate for 1 hour before serving. Store in a ziplock plastic bag in the refrigerator for up to 3 weeks.

S'mores for Me Dip

Who doesn't love a melty, gooey, deliciously warm s'more? Here's a way to bring this campfire treat to your kitchen, no flame required! I recommend using Enjoy Life chocolate chips and homemade marshmallows for this recipe. If you do not have time to make marshmallows, Public Goods is an excellent option; I also like Target's Good & Gather brand. Both are free of artificial colors, flavors, and preservatives.

Serves 4 to 6

1 cup chocolate chips

1 cup mini or regular marshmallows, homemade (page 225) or store-bought

8 gluten-free graham crackers or 2 to 3 cups Simple Mills Honey Cinnamon Sweet Thins

1 In a 7-inch springform pan, layer ½ cup of the chocolate chips and ½ cup of the marshmallows, then repeat the layers.

2 Place the pan in the basket of a 5.3-quart air fryer and air fry for 5 to 6 minutes at 350°F.

3 Carefully remove the dish and serve with the graham crackers.

Make-Your-Own Mallows

Did you know that making marshmallows is actually pretty darn easy? Store-bought marshmallows are chock-full of dyes, preservatives, highly refined sugars, and other gut irritants, but homemade marshmallows are actually good for you!

Makes 24

2 to 3 tablespoons arrowroot powder

1 cup water

2 tablespoons unflavored gelatin

1 cup raw honey

1 teaspoon pure vanilla extract

Avocado oil, for greasing

1   Line a rimmed baking sheet with parchment paper and sprinkle 1 tablespoon of the arrowroot powder evenly over the surface.

2   In the bowl of a stand mixer, combine ½ cup of the water and sprinkle the gelatin over the top. Let sit for 10 minutes.

3   In a saucepan, combine the remaining ½ cup water and the honey. Bring to a boil over medium-high heat and let boil for 15 minutes, or until a candy thermometer reads 240°F.

4   Attach the whisk attachment to the mixer and turn it to low. While running, slowly drizzle the honey syrup down the side of the bowl. Then add the vanilla and increase the speed to medium-high. Let it mix for 8 to 10 minutes. The mixture will turn from brown to white and triple in volume.

5   Working quickly, spread the marshmallow cream on the prepared baking sheet and smooth with a silicone spatula. Allow it to cool and set at room temperature for 6 hours.

6   Gently rub the tops of the marshmallows with 1 tablespoon arrowroot powder. Grease a sharp knife with oil and slice the marshmallows into 24 pieces. If the marshmallows are still sticky, toss them in the remaining 1 tablespoon arrowroot powder to coat. Store in an airtight container at room temperature for up to 1 month.

Caramel Chocolate Turtles

During my childhood, chocolate turtles were one of my mom's favorite candies and a delicacy we kids were not often allowed to eat, as they were quite pricey. As an adult, I still opt not to consume the store-bought candy, not just because of the price but because of the ingredients as well. Instead, I make my own at home. They're just as delicious without the price tag. A perfect afternoon pick-me-up!

Makes 10

5 pitted Medjool dates, cut in half

2 tablespoons Ooey-Goocy Caramel (page 227) or peanut butter

30 pecan halves, 10 for the turtle heads and 20 cut in half lengthwise for the limbs

⅓ cup chocolate chips

Fine sea salt, for sprinkling

1 Line a rimmed baking sheet with parchment paper.

2 Smash each date half into a flattened disk using your fingers. Place them on the prepared baking sheet. Add a thin layer of caramel over the top. Position 1 full pecan on each as the head and 4 thin pecan pieces as the arms and legs.

3 Melt the chocolate chips in the microwave, stopping to stir every 30 seconds to ensure the chocolate melts without burning. Spoon the chocolate over the bodies of the turtles, then top with a sprinkle of salt.

4 Refrigerate for 30 minutes to allow the caramel and chocolate to set. Store in an airtight container in the fridge for up to 2 weeks.

Ooey-Gooey Caramel

This dreamy, dairy-free sauce comes together in seconds and consists of just three ingredients. It's a great, inexpensive alternative to store-bought sauces that can be packed full of stabilizers and corn syrup. Use it to top ice cream or pancakes, or make my cute Caramel Chocolate Turtles (page 226) or Dairy-Free Tres Leches cake (page 229)! If you cannot consume sesame seeds, use almond butter or sunflower seed butter instead of tahini.

Makes ¼ cup

2 tablespoons avocado oil

2 tablespoons 100% pure maple syrup

1 tablespoon tahini, homemade (page 239) or store-bought

In a small bowl, combine all of the ingredients and stir until smooth. Store in an airtight container in the refrigerator for up to 1 month.

Dairy-Free Tres Leches

My favorite cake mix to use for this recipe is Pamela's, which you can find at Whole Foods Market or Sprouts. I highly recommend So Delicious coconut whipped cream as the cake topper. This is a very easy recipe to throw together for a gathering. It's incredibly delicious—you've been warned!

Serves 12

¼ cup unsweetened vanilla almond (or other) milk, homemade (page 234) or store-bought

¼ cup canned full-fat coconut milk

¼ cup Ooey-Gooey Caramel (page 227)

1 gluten-free vanilla cake, made according to the mix package instructions

6 ounces coconut whipped cream

½ cup unsweetened coconut flakes

2 tablespoons slivered almonds

Ground cinnamon, for topping

1 In a small saucepan, combine the almond milk, coconut milk, and 3 tablespoons of the caramel and warm over medium heat until smooth.

2 Using a fork, poke holes all over the top of the vanilla cake. Slowly pour the warm milk mixture over the top, making sure to pour all around, including in the holes and near the edges. Refrigerate the cake, uncovered, for at least 1 hour or overnight to allow it to absorb the milk.

3 Frost the cake with the whipped cream and top with the coconut flakes, slivered almonds, remaining 1 tablespoon caramel, and a sprinkle of cinnamon.

Tropical Fruit Skewers with Caramel Drizzle

This is such a great treat to make for a picky-platter lunch! Serve slices of turkey, cheese, carrots, celery, broccoli, and cherry tomatoes with a side of Creamy Ranch Dressing (page 153). The fruit is definitely the star of the show, and my kids love to skewer it for me and make the caramel sauce. I've found that getting them involved in the cooking process made the transition from a more heavily processed food diet to a natural food diet a little easier. It helps that this fruit tastes like dessert!

Serves 4 to 8

FOR THE CARAMEL

8 large pitted Medjool dates

½ cup canned full-fat coconut milk

¼ cup unsweetened almond (or other) milk, homemade (page 234) or store-bought

2 tablespoons 100% pure maple syrup

¼ teaspoon fine sea salt

FOR THE SKEWERS

2 cups fresh pineapple, cut into 1-inch pieces

2 medium bananas, peeled and cut into 1-inch pieces

1 large ripe mango, peeled, pitted, and cut into 1-inch pieces

1 tablespoon melted coconut oil

2 tablespoons unsweetened shredded coconut

1   Preheat the oven broiler.

2   Combine the dates, coconut milk, almond milk, maple syrup, and salt in a high-powered blender. Blend on high, scraping the sides as needed, until the sauce is smooth. Set aside.

3   Thread the pieces of pineapple, banana, and mango on 8 wooden or metal skewers. Place the skewers on a rimmed baking sheet pan.

4   Brush each skewer with melted coconut oil and sprinkle with shredded coconut on all sides. Broil for 2 minutes, or until the coconut has toasted. Flip the skewers over and cook for an additional 2 to 3 minutes.

5   Transfer the skewers to a serving platter and drizzle with the caramel sauce.

Make-at-Home Money Savers

Almond Butter Almond
   Milk 234

Taco Seasoning. 234

Garam Masala. 236

Jerk Seasoning 237

Cajun Seasoning. 238

Italian Seasoning 238

Easy Three-Ingredient
   Tahini 239

Homemade Mayo 240

Tangy Barbecue Sauce . . 241

Homemade Bone Broth . . 243

Vegetable Broth 244

Classic Italian
   Dressing 246

Almond Butter Almond Milk

No more straining through a nut milk bag—this almond butter almond milk hack is going to save you a bundle of time and money! Store-bought almond milk is typically full of stabilizers, gums, and emulsifiers. Making your own at home isn't just a money saver but a gut saver too. Just make sure that the almond butter you're using contains only almonds (and maybe salt)!

If you're not using a high-powered blender, omit the date and opt for 2 teaspoons of date syrup instead!

Makes 1 quart

4 cups water
¼ cup organic almond butter
1 teaspoon pure vanilla extract
1 pitted Medjool date

Combine all of the ingredients in a high-powered blender and blend until combined, about 30 seconds. Store in an airtight container in the refrigerator for up to 6 days.

Taco Seasoning

Make your own taco seasoning at home! Store-bought brands can have added sugar, preservatives, and fillers. This homemade seasoning is just as delicious as the commercial stuff and more cost-effective too!

Makes 1 cup

⅓ cup chili powder
2½ tablespoons dried minced onion
4 teaspoons garlic powder
4 teaspoons ground cumin
4 teaspoons fine sea salt
2 teaspoons cayenne pepper
2 teaspoons paprika

In a small, wide-mouth jar, combine all of the ingredients. Screw the lid on tightly, then shake to combine.

Garam Masala

This is an aromatic blend of Indian spices. *Garam* means "hot" and *masala* means "spices," referring to the warm flavors of the ingredients, like cinnamon and cumin.

Makes ¼ cup

1 tablespoon ground cumin

1½ teaspoons ground coriander

1½ teaspoons ground cardamom

1½ teaspoons ground black pepper

1 teaspoon ground cinnamon

½ teaspoon ground cloves

½ teaspoon ground nutmeg

Combine all of the ingredients in a small, wide-mouth jar. Screw the lid on tightly, then shake to combine.

Jerk Seasoning

Jerking is a term used for the style of original Jamaican cooking where one pokes holes into meat so it can be permeated with more flavor from the seasoning. *Jerk* eventually became associated with a traditional spice rub.

1 tablespoon onion powder

1 tablespoon garlic powder

2 teaspoons cayenne pepper

2 teaspoons fine sea salt

2 teaspoons ground black pepper

2 teaspoons dried thyme

2 teaspoons coconut sugar or brown sugar

1 teaspoon ground allspice

1 teaspoon dried parsley

1 teaspoon paprika

½ teaspoon red pepper flakes

½ teaspoon ground cinnamon

½ teaspoon ground nutmeg

½ teaspoon ground cloves

¼ teaspoon ground cumin

Combine all of the ingredients in a small, wide-mouth jar. Screw the lid on tightly, then shake to combine.

Cajun Seasoning

Add this Cajun seasoning to anything for a delicious Southern kick! It's bold and packed with flavor, and I love it on shrimp, chicken, or pasta dishes.

Makes ¼ cup

2½ teaspoons smoked paprika

2 teaspoons fine sea salt

2 teaspoons garlic powder

1¼ teaspoons dried oregano

1¼ teaspoons dried thyme

1 teaspoon ground black pepper

1 teaspoon cayenne pepper

½ teaspoon red pepper flakes

Combine all of the ingredients in a small, wide-mouth jar. Screw the lid on tightly, then shake to combine.

Italian Seasoning

I never purchase seasoning blends because they typically come with anti-caking agents and often a dose of added MSG. Use this homemade blend instead—no one will know the difference!

Makes ½ cup

2 tablespoons dried basil

2 tablespoons dried oregano

2 tablespoons dried parsley

1 tablespoon dried thyme

1 tablespoon dried rosemary

1 tablespoon red pepper flakes

1 teaspoon garlic powder

1 teaspoon dried minced onion

Combine all of the ingredients in a small, wide-mouth jar. Screw the lid on tightly, then shake to combine.

Easy Three-Ingredient Tahini

Tahini is a delicious sesame seed paste that can be used in any recipe that calls for peanut or almond butter. You can add a little bit of your favorite sweetener if you like.

If you have a wide-base blender or a large food processor, you'll want to double the recipe so that nothing gets trapped beneath the blades.

Makes 1 cup

2 cups raw sesame seeds

5 tablespoons extra-virgin olive oil

¼ teaspoon fine sea salt

1 Preheat a cast-iron skillet over medium heat.

2 Add the sesame seeds to the skillet and toast them, using a wooden spoon to keep them circulating in the pan so they don't burn, until they have a nice, golden color, 2 to 3 minutes.

3 Transfer the seeds to a small food processor or blender. Add the oil and salt. Blend on high until smooth and creamy, about 2 minutes.

4 Store in a covered container in the refrigerator for up to 2 months.

Homemade Mayo

I put off making my own mayo for years! At first, the thought of it really intimidated me, but it's one of the easiest things that I make in my kitchen. To ensure foolproof mayo, you'll use an immersion blender, a jar that fits the head of your immersion blender pretty snugly, and a few simple ingredients.

It is important that you use a lighter oil, like avocado oil or light olive oil, as extra-virgin olive oil is too heavy and creates an undesirable flavor.

Makes 1½ cups

1 large egg

1¼ cups avocado oil, light olive oil, or other light-tasting oil

1½ teaspoons yellow mustard

1 teaspoon apple cider vinegar

1 teaspoon fresh lemon juice

½ teaspoon fine sea salt

⅛ teaspoon raw honey or other sweetener

1 Combine all of the ingredients, in order, in a wide-mouth jar.

2 Submerge the head of an immersion blender in the jar and begin to pulse the ingredients on the lowest setting. Do not move the head up and down; just keep it still. When the mixture begins to emulsify, slowly draw the head of the blender upward to begin to incorporate the oil that is separated on the top. Keep blending until the mayo has fully combined.

3 Store in an airtight container in the refrigerator for up to 2 weeks.

Tangy Barbecue Sauce

Our family loves barbecue sauce. Unfortunately, most of the sauces sold in stores have artificial colors and highly refined sugars. No problem, because it turns out barbecue sauce is easy to make at home! To be more efficient, I recommend making a big batch, freezing portions in a muffin pan, and transferring to a freezer bag. This way, you have a small amount on hand whenever you need it.

Makes 2½ cups

1 (15-ounce) can tomato sauce

2 tablespoons coconut sugar

2 tablespoons raw honey

1 tablespoon apple cider vinegar

1½ teaspoons Worcestershire sauce

1½ teaspoons Dijon mustard

1 clove garlic, minced

½ teaspoon dried oregano

½ teaspoon chili powder

½ teaspoon ground black pepper

1   Combine all of the ingredients in a small saucepan. Bring to a boil over medium-high heat, stirring occasionally.

2   Turn the heat down to a simmer and cook, stirring occasionally so nothing burns on the bottom, for 5 minutes.

3   Remove from the heat and let cool to room temperature. Store in an airtight container in the refrigerator for up to 2 weeks.

Homemade Bone Broth

Low-sodium, sugar-free bone broths can be difficult to find in the grocery store for less than $6 a carton. Since bone broth is a base for many soups and other dishes, this makes things much more expensive than they need to be. A few years ago, I decided to begin making my own broths at home in an electric pressure cooker. Not only is it a big budget saver, but it's also a great way to have a lower-waste kitchen. I toss in vegetables that are on their way out and leftover bones from cooked chicken, beef, lamb, or pork.

Makes 4 quarts

3 pounds meaty bones of choice (from raw or cooked chicken, beef, lamb, or pork)

4 quarts water

4 stalks celery, diced

2 large carrots, diced

1 medium yellow onion, thinly sliced

¼ cup fresh parsley

1 tablespoon apple cider vinegar

1 teaspoon fine sea salt

1　Combine all of the ingredients in an electric pressure cooker.

2　Place the lid on the cooker and make sure the vent valve is in the **SEALING** position. Select the **MANUAL/ PRESSURE COOK** function, **HIGH PRESSURE**, and use the +/- buttons until the display reads 90 minutes.

3　When the cooker beeps, let it naturally release the pressure (this should take about 25 minutes).

4　Once the liquid has cooled to warm or room temperature, carefully strain through a fine-mesh strainer into a bowl. Discard the bones and vegetables. Ladle the broth into quart-size glass jars.

5　Cover and store in the refrigerator for up to 6 days, or freeze in tempered glass jars (with at least 2 inches of space at the top) for up to 6 months.

Vegetable Broth

This is one of my favorite Instant Loss recipes of all time! It's certainly one I make the most frequently. Simply collect your kitchen vegetable scraps, clean them well, and freeze them in a ziplock freezer bag until the bag is full and you're ready to make this staple. If you don't have time to accumulate scraps, simple use 4 cups roughly chopped vegetables—mainly carrots, celery, and onions.

Makes 4 quarts

4 cups vegetable scraps (onion ends, carrot tops, celery ends, bell pepper tops, sweet potato ends, etc.)

4 quarts water

5 cloves garlic, crushed

1 bay leaf

1 tablespoon dried parsley flakes

1 tablespoon extra-virgin olive oil

1 teaspoon dried rosemary

1 teaspoon dried thyme

½ teaspoon fine sea salt

¼ teaspoon ground black pepper

1 Combine all of the ingredients in an electric pressure cooker.

2 Place the lid on the cooker and make sure the vent valve is in the **SEALING** position. Select the **MANUAL/PRESSURE COOK** function, **HIGH PRESSURE**, and use the +/- buttons until the display reads 40 minutes.

3 When the cooker beeps, let it naturally release the pressure (this should take about 25 minutes).

4 Once the liquid has cooled to warm or room temperature, carefully strain through a fine-mesh strainer into a bowl. Discard the vegetable scraps and bay leaf. Ladle the broth into quart-size glass jars.

5 Cover and store in the refrigerator for up to 6 days, or freeze in tempered glass jars (with at least 2 inches of space at the top) for up to 6 months.

Classic Italian Dressing

I have such a struggle in the dressing aisle at the store. The stuff that's affordable is full of processed sugars, hydrogenated oils, and tons of preservatives. The stuff with great ingredients can be $6 a bottle or more. This prompted me to begin making my own dressings. It's easier than you'd think, usually requiring only a spoon or whisk and a bowl. Or, if you like your dressing a bit thicker and emulsified, an immersion blender yields beautiful results!

Makes 1 cup

¾ cup extra-virgin olive oil

3 tablespoons red wine vinegar

1 teaspoon 100% pure maple syrup

1 teaspoon dried minced onion

1 teaspoon dried oregano

1 teaspoon fine sea salt

½ teaspoon garlic powder

½ teaspoon dried parsley flakes

¼ teaspoon dried basil

¼ teaspoon ground black pepper

⅛ teaspoon dried thyme

Combine all of the ingredients in a small, wide-mouth jar and blend using an immersion blender until smooth. Store in an airtight container in the refrigerator for up to 2 weeks. Shake well before using.

Acknowledgments

Instant Loss fam, I can hardly believe that this is our fifth book together. If I hadn't spent the last six years of my life writing the books, I don't know if I would believe that number myself. I am living proof and testimony of what other people's belief in you can do, but here's the trick . . .

You have to believe it too.

Someone once told me to believe people when they tell you what you're good at. It sounds simple, but for most of us, it's really hard to do. It's easier to listen to the voices that undermine the positive things. The ones that oppress and keep you small. I decided years ago that when people give me a compliment that I'd stop trying to undermine their praise with excuses or explanations about how I'm really not so great and that I'd simply respond: "Thank you."

It was moving forward, armed with this new perspective, that did indeed shift my perspective. The things we've accomplished together, the things that I've accomplished over these last seven years, can be defined by a number of words but they have truly been *great*.

And they've been great because for some reason, God decided I get to be the luckiest woman in the world and attract all of these *great* individuals to myself. There is, of course, you—my fairy godmothers. Those who saw me for what I could be when I was still a caterpillar. You guided and taught me, instructed and loved me, and then you showed up with unwavering support again and again.

There's my beautiful, grizzly bearded husband, Brady, and our infinitely amazing trio of babies who are not really babies anymore—we're headed into the teenager years now. But I still think of you as my babies. Your omnipresence in my life has been a steadfast support and my greatest inspiration. If not for you, I'd have no reason to cook or create or be a wife or a mom. You are so interwoven into the depths of my identity, there's no separating us anymore.

We were driving home last night when I got a notification on Facebook about Brady's and my fourteenth Facebook Friendaversary. Brady said, "It seems longer than that, though, doesn't it? Like you've been with me my whole life. Even when I was a kid; even when you weren't, I still feel like you were." And without realizing it, he gifted me with the most beautiful way to sum us up. Even when I didn't love you, Brady, I did. Even when you weren't with me, you were.

To my family, which encompasses quite a lot of people so for the sake of brevity and not leaving anyone out—you were my earliest teachers and most positive cheerleaders. You never saw me as anything but great from the beginning. A perk of being the oldest, no doubt, but nevertheless. I always felt special, like I was meant for something humungous, and it was your complete confidence in me that did that. And it's brought me so far. Mom, Dad, Grandma and Grandpa, Grandma Sharon, the Aunt Kims, Colin, Kyle, Bethany, Connor, Caleb, Tristan—and so many more. I'm so glad that it was your family that I got to be part of.

My girls—Heather, Janna, Katie, Sloane, Shaylee, Courtney—this has been quite the year for all of us. As struggles abound we're always there to see each other through. You are my lifers, my FBI detectives, my totally uncensored sisters, my ride or dies, the ones I'm growing old with. Thank you for being the keepers of my confidence, the ones who knock me upside the head and tell me to get right with my husband and God, for the real real on momlife, and for understanding that I'm always the wife in our relationship. For always having the hot goss and making me feel like I'm forever twenty-one, I love you more than words can say.

Lisa, thank you for helping bring fresh new ideas and creativity to my brain! I always have the best time troubleshooting and talking things through with you. You've been an invaluable presence for me since the first book and I am so grateful!

Andy, I struck gold when you slid into my DMs. I knew right away that I wouldn't be able to do a book without you, and I was right. Thank you for investing so much of your time into molding and shaping me into an author. Your resources, connections, and know-how have been vital assets and have taken me so far. I love you so much.

The HarperCollins team: Sarah, Tai, Emma, and Karen. There's no way that a project like this comes together without a very talented group of individuals. Editors, proofreader, copyeditor, legal reader, cover art and layout designers, sales and publicity—I am so fortunate that I do not have to wear all of those hats. You guys make my life so much easier, and I am beyond grateful for all of the hard work and dedication you've put into making my dreams a reality. We made another book!! Ah!

My photography team: Ghazalle, Vanessa, Vivian, EJ, Mateo, and Sydney. You are my comrades in arms. I feel like this book is just as much yours as it is mine. Thank you for transforming the downstairs of my house into a studio so that I could easily have my family be part of every recipe and moment. I cherish our times together: afternoon tea, date o'clock, electrolytes, broken Vitamix pitchers, and floors. It was pure joy to have every single one of you warm my kitchen. I still have our photowall intact, I don't have the heart to take it down. I am so proud of the stunning book we've created. Thank you, with all of my heart.

So . . . if I am great at all, it is only because of all of you. I'm so fortunate that I get to do life with the greatest of the great.

Index

Note: Page references in *italics* indicate photographs.

A

Air fryer, 42
Almond Cake Shake, *56,* 57
Almond flour, 33
Almond Milk
  Almond Butter, 234
  preparing, 18
Apples
  The Best Darn Green Juice, *48,* 49
  Sangria Smoothie, 50
Aquafaba, 31
Arrowroot powder, 34
Avocados
  Blueberry Kale Spring Green Salad, 98, *99*
  Citrus Chicken Salad, 92, *93*
  Cobb Salad with Chicken Strips and Honey Mustard, *100,* 101

B

Bacon
  Cobb Salad with Chicken Strips and Honey Mustard, *100,* 101
  Easy Egg Bite Casserole, 201
  Sweet Potato Frittata, *70,* 71
Baking sheets, 44
Banana(s)
  Almond Cake Shake, *56,* 57
  Blueberry Meal Replacement Smoothie, 55

Bread, The Best Gluten-Free, 60, *61*
Creamy Peach-Orange Smoothie, 51
Strawberry Shortcake Smoothie, 52, *53*
Tropical Fruit Skewers with Caramel Drizzle, *230,* 231
Bang Bang Beef Lettuce Cups, *154,* 155–56
Bang Bang Chicken, *148,* 149
Bang Bang Sauce, *154,* 156
Barbecue Chicken Sandwiches, 158, *159*
Barbecue Sauce, Tangy, 241
Basil
  Edamame Pesto Rotini, 120, *121*
  Spaghetti Squash Lasagna Casserole, 203–4
Bean(s). *See also* Edamame
  Beefy Enchilada Skillet, 210, *211*
  The Best-Ever Cabbage Soup, 126
  Black, and Mango Stew, Caribbean, 86
  Cauliflower Tinga Tacos, 202
  Deconstructed Stuffed Pepper Bowls, 183
  electric pressure cooker cook times, 21
  Green, and Chicken, Creamy Ranch, 152–53

and Herb Salad, Mediterranean, 94
Jalapeño Popper Chicken Chili, 84, *85*
Red, Jollof Rice with, 130
Red Chile Tostada, 140
and Rice Burritos, 137
Taco Chicken, 176
3-, Turkey Chili, 160
Beef
  antibiotic-free, 40
  Bang Bang, Lettuce Cups, *154,* 155–56
  Beefy Enchilada Skillet, 210, *211*
  electric pressure cooker cook times, 21
  grass-fed, 40
  grass-finished, 40
  Hamburger Tacos, *212,* 213
  hormone-free, 40
  Italian Wedding Soup, *88,* 89
  Philly Steak Stir-Fry, *162,* 163
  Swedish Meatballs, 195
Beet Bisque, Creamy, 78
Berry(ies)
  Banana Blueberry Meal Replacement Smoothie, 55
  Blueberry Chia Seed Muffins, 68, *69*
  Blueberry Kale Spring Green Salad, 98, *99*
  Blueberry Spring Green Salad, 98, *99*
  Lemon Skillet Cake, Old-Fashioned, 64, *65*

Berry(ies) (*continued*)
  Mini Maple Vanilla Nut
    Cakes, *216,* 217
  Strawberry Shortcake
    Smoothie, 52, *53*
  Summer, Limeade, 51
Blender, 42
Blueberry
  Banana Meal Replacement
    Smoothie, 55
  Chia Seed Muffins, 68, *69*
  Kale Spring Green Salad,
    98, *99*
Bone Broth, Homemade, 243
Bread. *See also* Tortillas
  Banana, The Best Gluten-
    Free, 60, *61*
  Pulled BBQ Mushrooms on
    Toast, 127
Broccoli
  Chicken Alfredo, *190,* 191
  electric pressure cooker
    cook times, 21
  Simple Chicken Sausage
    Sheet Pan, 205
  Steamed, The Easiest,
    110
Broth
  Bone, Homemade, 243
  Vegetable, 244
Brussels sprouts
  Blueberry Kale Spring
    Green Salad, 98, *99*
  electric pressure cooker
    cook times, 21
Buffalo Chicken Wraps, 176
Burritos, Bean and Rice, 137

C
Cabbage
  Egg Roll in a Bowl with
    Sriracha Mayo, 196, *197*

electric pressure cooker
    cook times, 21
  Pulled BBQ Mushrooms on
    Toast, 127
  Soup, The Best-Ever, 126
  Thai Peanut Chicken Salad,
    105
Caesar Salad, Classic, *102,*
    103
Cajun Seasoning, *235,* 238
Cakes
  Carrot, with Cashew Cream
    Frosting, 220–22, *221*
  Dairy-Free Tres Leches,
    228, 229
  Lemon Berry Skillet, Old-
    Fashioned, 64, *65*
  Mini Maple Vanilla Nut,
    216, 217
Calories, counting, 4–6
Caramel
  Chocolate Turtles, 226
  Drizzle, Tropical Fruit
    Skewers with, *230,* 231
  Ooey-Gooey, 227
Carrot(s)
  Cake with Cashew Cream
    Frosting, 220–22,
    221
  Dogs, *132,* 133
  electric pressure cooker
    cook times, 21
  Honey Harissa, 114, *115*
  Summertime Veggie Salad
    with Lemon Tahini
    Dressing, 96, *97*
  Thai Peanut Chicken Salad,
    105
Cashew Cream Cheese
  Frosting, *221,* 222
Cashew milk, preparing, 18
Cassava flour, 34

Cauliflower
  electric pressure cooker
    cook times, 21
  Garlic Mashed, 113
  Grits and Southern Shrimp,
    62, *63*
  Tinga Tacos, 202
Certified humane, defined, 40
Cheese
  Air-Fryer Mini Pepperoni
    Pizza, 171
  Beefy Enchilada Skillet,
    210, *211*
  Classic Caesar Salad, *102,*
    103
  Classic Tuna Melts, *178,* 179
  Easy Egg Bite Casserole, 201
  Green Chile Chicken
    Enchiladas, 200
  Lightened-Up Turkey
    Reuben, 144, *145*
  Pepperoni Zucchini Pizza,
    141
  Spaghetti Squash Lasagna
    Casserole, 203–4
  Turkey Parm Meatloaf
    Minis, 161
Chia Seed
  Blueberry Muffins, 68, *69*
  Pudding, The Best, 73
Chicken
  Adobo, Filipino, 157
  Bang Bang, *148,* 149
  Barbecue, Sandwiches, 158,
    159
  Broccoli Alfredo, *190,* 191
  Buffalo, Wraps, 176
  Chili, Jalapeño Popper, 84,
    85
  Curry, Stir-Fry, 172, *173*
  electric pressure cooker
    cook times, 21

Enchilada Roll-Ups, 182
Enchiladas, Green Chile, 200
free-range, 40
and Green Beans, Creamy
    Ranch, 152–53
Legs, Szechuan Honey, 166
Mango Salad, Herby, 95
organic, 41
pasture-raised, 41
Peanut Salad, Thai, 105
Pot Pie Soup, 87
Ramen, Easy, *192,* 193–94
Salad, 13
Salad, Citrus, 92, *93*
Schnitzel, Oven-Baked,
    with Fries, 206, *207*
Sheet Pan Fajitas, 208, *209*
Soup, Greek Lemon-Dill,
    76, 77
Stew, Ginger-Turmeric,
    80–81
Strips, Gluten-Free, 177
Strips and Honey Mustard,
    Cobb Salad with, *100,* 101
Taco, 176
Chicken Sausage Sheet Pan,
    Simple, 205
Chickpea flour, 33
Chickpea(s)
    Cauliflower Tinga Tacos,
        202
    electric pressure cooker
        cook times, 21
Chili
    3-Bean Turkey, 160
    Jalapeño Popper Chicken,
        84, *85*
Chili powder
    Taco Seasoning, 234, *235*
Chocolate
    Almond Cake Shake, *56,* 57
    The Best Pancakes Ever, 66

Caramel Turtles, 226
Peanut Butter Baked Oats,
    72
Peanut Butter Crispy Rice
    Treats, 223
S'mores for Me Dip, 224
Chowder, Salmon, 79
Cobb Salad with Chicken
    Strips and Honey
    Mustard, *100,* 101
Coconut
    Almond Cake Shake, *56,* 57
    Dairy-Free Tres Leches,
        228, 229
    -Lime Curry Sauce, Mussels
        in, 184, *185*
    Red Lentil Dal with
        Spinach, 124, *125*
    Tropical Fruit Skewers
        with Caramel Drizzle,
        230, 231
Coconut flour, 34
Coconut milk, preparing, 18
Coconut sugar, 37
Corn
    and Cucumber Salad, Zesty
        Herby, 142, *143*
    Deconstructed Stuffed
        Pepper Bowls, 183
    electric pressure cooker
        cook times, 21
    Taco Chicken, 176
Cucumber(s)
    The Best Darn Green Juice,
        48, 49
    Citrus Fruit Cooler, 55
    and Corn Salad, Zesty
        Herby, 142, *143*
    Mediterranean Herb and
        Bean Salad, 94
    Salad, Chinese-Style,
        104

Teriyaki Salmon Rice
    Bowls, 146, *147*
Tzatziki Sauce, *164,* 165
Cumin
    Garam Masala, *235,* 236
Curry Chicken Stir-Fry, 172,
    173
Curry Sauce, Coconut-Lime,
    Mussels in, 184, *185*

D
Dates
    Almond Cake Shake, *56,* 57
    Caramel Chocolate Turtles,
        226
    Summer Berry Limeade, 51
    Tropical Fruit Skewers
        with Caramel Drizzle,
        230, 231
Desserts
    Caramel Chocolate Turtles,
        226
    Carrot Cake with Cashew
        Cream Frosting, 220–22,
        221
    Dairy-Free Tres Leches,
        228, 229
    Make-Your-Own Mallows,
        225
    Mini Maple Vanilla Nut
        Cakes, *216,* 217
    Ooey-Gooey Caramel, 227
    Peanut Butter Chocolate
        Crispy Rice Treats, 223
    Rice Pudding Sundae, 218,
        219
    S'mores for Me Dip, 224
    Tropical Fruit Skewers
        with Caramel Drizzle,
        230, 231
Dip, S'mores for Me, 224
Dirty Dozen and Clean 15, 40

Dressings
    Creamy Ranch, 153
    Italian, Classic, 246
    Thousand Island, 144
Drinks
    Almond Cake Shake, *56, 57*
    Banana Blueberry Meal
        Replacement Smoothie,
        55 .
    The Best Darn Green Juice,
        48, 49
    Citrus Fruit Cooler, 55
    Creamy Peach-Orange
        Smoothie, 51
    Sangria Smoothie, 50
    Strawberry Shortcake
        Smoothie, 52, *53*
    Summer Berry Limeade, 51
    Tropical Greens, 50

E
Edamame
    and Greens, Sesame Peanut
        Noodles with, 136
    Pesto Rotini, 120, *121*
    Thai Peanut Chicken Salad,
        105
Eggplant, Roasted, with
        Lemon-Dill Tahini and
        Paprika Vinaigrette, *122,*
        123
Egg Roll in a Bowl with
        Sriracha Mayo, 196, *197*
Egg(s)
    buying, labels on, 40–41
    Cobb Salad with Chicken
        Strips and Honey
        Mustard, *100,* 101
    Easy Chicken Ramen, *192,*
        193–94
    Easy Egg Bite Casserole,
        201

electric pressure cooker
        cook times, 22
    for recipes, 31
    Red Chile Tostada, 140
    Salad, 13
    Soft-Boiled, *192, 194*
    substitutes, 31
    Sweet Potato Frittata, *70,* 71
Electric pressure cooker, 42
Enchiladas, Green Chile
        Chicken, 200
Ethically raised, defined, 40

F
Fajitas, Sheet Pan, 208, *209*
Fats, healthy, 6, 31–33
Fig, Dried, and Pecan
        Oatmeal, 67
Fish
    Classic Tuna Melts, *178,* 179
    electric pressure cooker
        cook times, 21
    farm-raised, 41
    One-Pot Air-Fryer Salmon
        and Potatoes, 174, *175*
    Salmon Chowder, 79
    sustainably sourced, 41
    Teriyaki Salmon Rice
        Bowls, 146, *147*
    Tuna Pasta Salad, 186, *187*
    Tuna Salad, 13
    wild-caught, 41
Flax eggs, 31
Flours, alternative, 33–34
Food processor, 44
Frittata, Sweet Potato, *70,* 71
Frosting, Cashew Cream
        Cheese, *221,* 222
Fruit. See also specific fruits
    Citrus, Cooler, 55
    organic/conventionally
        grown/raised, 38–41

portion sizes, 6
    Tropical, Skewers with
        Caramel Drizzle, *230,* 231

G
Garam Masala, *235,* 236
Garlic Mashed Cauliflower, 113
Ginger-Turmeric Chicken
        Stew, 80–81
GMOs, 38
Grab-on-the-go foods, 14
Graham crackers
    S'mores for Me Dip, 224
Grains. *See also* Oats; Quinoa;
        Rice
    electric pressure cooker
        cook times, 22
Grapefruit
    Citrus Fruit Cooler, 55
Grapes
    Sangria Smoothie, 50
Green Beans
    and Chicken, Creamy
        Ranch, 152–53
    electric pressure cooker
        cook times, 21
Green Juice, The Best Darn,
        48, 49
Greens. See also specific
        greens
    Citrus Chicken Salad, 92, *93*
    Cobb Salad with Chicken
        Strips and Honey
        Mustard, *100,* 101
    and Edamame, Sesame
        Peanut Noodles with, 136
    Simple Salad, 14

H
Hamburger Tacos, *212,* 213
Harissa Honey Carrots, 114,
        115

Hemp seed milk, preparing, 18
Herbs. *See also* Basil
    Herby Mango Chicken
        Salad, 95
    Italian Seasoning, *235, 238*
Honey
    Chicken Legs, Szechuan,
        166
    Harissa Carrots, 114, *115*
    raw, about, 37
Hot sauce
    Strip Sauce, 177

I

Immersion blender, 42
Ingredients, 31–37

J

Jerk Seasoning, *235, 237*
Jollof Rice with Red Beans, 130
Juice
    Citrus Fruit Cooler, 55
    Green, The Best Darn, *48,*
        49
Juicer, 42

K

Kale
    Banana Blueberry Meal
        Replacement Smoothie,
        55
    The Best Darn Green Juice,
        48, 49
    Blueberry Spring Green
        Salad, 98, *99*
Kitchen tools, 42–44
Knives, 44

L

Lemon
    Berry Skillet Cake, Old-
        Fashioned, 64, *65*

Citrus Fruit Cooler, 55
    -Dill Tahini and Paprika
        Vinaigrette, Roasted
        Eggplant with, *122,* 123
    Tahini Dressing,
        Summertime Veggie
        Salad with, 96, *97*
Lentil(s)
    electric pressure cooker
        cook times, 21
    Red, Coconut Dal with
        Spinach, 124, *125*
    Summertime Veggie Salad
        with Lemon Tahini
        Dressing, 96, *97*
Lettuce
    Classic Caesar Salad, *102,*
        103
    Cups, Bang Bang Beef, *154,*
        155–56
    Zesty Herby Corn and
        Cucumber Salad, 142, *143*
Lime
    Citrus Fruit Cooler, 55
    Summer Berry Limeade, 51

M

Mango
    and Black Bean Stew,
        Caribbean, 86
    Chicken Salad, Herby, 95
    Tropical Fruit Skewers
        with Caramel Drizzle,
        230, 231
    Tropical Greens, 50
Maple syrup, 37
Maple Vanilla Nut Cakes,
    Mini, *216,* 217
Marinara, Penne Pasta, 170
Marshmallows
    Make-Your-Own Mallows,
        225

S'mores for Me Dip, 224
Mayonnaise
    Bang Bang Sauce, *154,*
        156
    Creamy Ranch Dressing,
        153
    Homemade Mayo, 240
    Sriracha Mayo, 196
    Strip Sauce, 177
Meal planning tips, 10–11
Meal plans, 25–29
Meat. *See also* Beef; Pork
    electric pressure cooker
        cook times, 21
    organic/conventionally
        grown/raised, 38–41
Meatballs, Swedish, 195
Meatloaf Minis, Turkey
    Parm, 161
Milks (nondairy)
    almond, 18
    Almond Butter Almond,
        234
    cashew, 18
    coconut, 18
    hemp seed, 18
    homemade, benefits of, 17
    oat, 18
Muffins, Blueberry Chia
    Seed, 68, *69*
Mushrooms
    Jerk, Creamy Jamaican-
        Style Pasta with, 128,
        129
    Philly Steak Stir-Fry, *162,*
        163
    Pulled BBQ, on Toast, 127
Mussels
    in Coconut-Lime Curry
        Sauce, 184, *185*
    electric pressure cooker
        cook times, 21

N

Noodles
　Easy Chicken Ramen, *192,*
　　193–94
　Sesame Peanut, with
　　Edamame and Greens,
　　136
Nutritional information, note
　on, 44–45
Nutritional yeast, 34–37
Nuts. *See also* Pecan(s);
　Walnuts
　Almond Cake Shake, *56,*
　　57
　Cashew Cream Cheese
　　Frosting, *221,* 222
　Honey Harissa Carrots, 114,
　　115
　preparing nondairy milk
　　with, 18

O

Oat flour, 34
Oat milk, preparing, 18
Oats
　Chocolate Peanut Butter
　　Baked, 72
　Dried Fig and Pecan
　　Oatmeal, 67
　electric pressure cooker
　　cook times, 22
Orange(s)
　Citrus Chicken Salad, 92,
　　93
　Citrus Fruit Cooler, 55
　-Peach Smoothie, Creamy,
　　51
　Sangria Smoothie, 50
　Tropical Greens, 50
Organic foods, 38–40

P

Pancakes, The Best Ever, 66
Paprika
　Cajun Seasoning, *235,* 238
　Vinaigrette and Lemon-Dill
　　Tahini, Roasted Eggplant
　　with, *122,* 123
Pasta
　Broccoli Chicken Alfredo,
　　190, 191
　Edamame Pesto Rotini,
　　120, *121*
　Italian Wedding Soup, *88,*
　　89
　with Jerk Mushrooms,
　　Creamy Jamaican-Style,
　　128, *129*
　Mussels in Coconut-Lime
　　Curry Sauce, 184, *185*
　Penne, Marinara, 170
　Rice Pilaf, 108, *109*
　Tuna Salad, 186, *187*
Peach-Orange Smoothie,
　Creamy, 51
Peanut Butter
　Chinese-Style Cucumber
　　Salad, 104
　Chocolate Baked Oats,
　　72
　Chocolate Crispy Rice
　　Treats, 223
　PB&J Rice Cake, 14
　Sesame Peanut Noodles
　　with Edamame and
　　Greens, 136
　Thai Peanut Chicken Salad,
　　105
Peanut Sesame Noodles with
　Edamame and Greens,
　136
Peas
　Tuna Pasta Salad, 186, *187*

Pecan(s)
　Caramel Chocolate Turtles,
　　226
　Carrot Cake with Cashew
　　Cream Frosting, 220–22,
　　221
　and Dried Fig Oatmeal, 67
Pepperoni
　Pizza, Air Fryer Mini, 171
　Zucchini Pizza, 141
Pepper(s)
　Chicken Enchilada Roll-
　　Ups, 182
　Creamy Jamaican-
　　Style Pasta with Jerk
　　Mushrooms, 128, *129*
　Deconstructed Stuffed,
　　Bowls, 183
　Easy Egg Bite Casserole,
　　201
　Jalapeño Popper Chicken
　　Chili, 84, *85*
　Jollof Rice with Red Beans,
　　130
　Philly Steak Stir-Fry, *162,*
　　163
　Sheet Pan Fajitas, 208, *209*
Pesto Edamame Rotini, 120,
　121
Pilaf, Rice, 108, *109*
Pineapple
　Sangria Smoothie, 50
　Tropical Fruit Skewers
　　with Caramel Drizzle,
　　230, 231
　Tropical Greens, 50
Pistachios
　Honey Harissa Carrots, 114,
　　115
Pizza
　Air Fryer Mini Pepperoni,
　　171

Pepperoni Zucchini, 141
Pork. *See also* Bacon
    Caribbean Mango and Black
       Bean Stew, 86
    Egg Roll in a Bowl with
       Sriracha Mayo, 196, *197*
    electric pressure cooker
       cook times, 21
    Souvlaki, Deconstructed,
       with Tzatziki Sauce, *164,*
       165
Portion sizes, 4–6
Potatoes. *See also* Sweet
    Potato(es)
    Buttery Mashed, 112
    electric pressure cooker
       cook times, 21
    Ginger-Turmeric Chicken
       Stew, 80–81
    Greek, *116,* 117
    Oven-Baked Chicken
       Schnitzel with Fries, 206,
       207
    and Salmon, One-Pot Air-
       Fryer, 174, *175*
    Salmon Chowder, 79
    Simple Chicken Sausage
       Sheet Pan, 205
Pots and pans, 44
Protein portion sizes, 6
Pudding
    Chia Seed, The Best, 73
    Rice, Sundae, 218, *219*
Pumpkin Bisque, 82, *83*

Q
Quick meals, 13–14
Quinoa
    Deconstructed Stuffed
       Pepper Bowls, 183
    electric pressure cooker
       cook times, 22

R
Ramen, Easy Chicken, *192,*
    193–94
Ranch Dressing, Creamy, 153
Rice
    and Bean Burritos, 137
    Bowls, Teriyaki Salmon,
       146, *147*
    Brown, Pressure Cooker,
       111
    electric pressure cooker
       cook times, 22
    Greek Lemon-Dill Chicken
       Soup, *76,* 77
    Jollof, with Red Beans,
       130
    Pilaf, 108, *109*
    Pudding Sundae, 218, *219*
Rice Cake, PB&J, 14
Rice Treats, Crispy, Peanut
    Butter Chocolate, 223

S
Salads
    Blueberry Kale Spring
       Green, 98, *99*
    Caesar, Classic, *102,* 103
    Chicken, 13
    Citrus Chicken, 92, *93*
    Cobb, with Chicken Strips
       and Honey Mustard, *100,*
       101
    Corn and Cucumber, Zesty
       Herby, 142, *143*
    Cucumber, Chinese-Style,
       104
    Egg, 13
    Herb and Bean,
       Mediterranean, 94
    Mango Chicken, Herby, 95
    Peanut Chicken, Thai, 105
    Simple, 14

Summertime Veggie, with
    Lemon Tahini Dressing,
    96, *97*
    Tuna, 13
    Tuna Pasta, 186, *187*
Salmon
    Chowder, 79
    and Potatoes, One-Pot Air-
       Fryer, 174, *175*
    Teriyaki, Rice Bowls, 146,
       147
Sandwiches
    Barbecue Chicken, 158, *159*
    Classic Tuna Melts, *178,* 179
    Lightened-Up Turkey
       Reuben, 144, *145*
Sangria Smoothie, 50
Sauces
    Bang Bang, *154,* 156
    Barbecue, Tangy, 241
    Ooey-Gooey Caramel, 227
    Strip, 177
    Tangy Barbecue Sauce, 241
    Teriyaki, 146
    Tzatziki, *164,* 165
Sauerkraut
    Barbecue Chicken
       Sandwiches, 158, *159*
    Lightened-Up Turkey
       Reuben, 144, *145*
Sausage, Chicken, Sheet Pan,
    Simple, 205
Seasonings
    Cajun, *235,* 238
    Garam Masala, *235,* 236
    Italian, *235,* 238
    Jerk, *235,* 237
    Taco, 234, *235*
Sesame seeds
    Easy Three-Ingredient
       Tahini, 239
Shake, Almond Cake, *56,* 57

Shellfish. *See* Mussels; Shrimp
Shrimp
    Pick-Up Garlicky Herb, with Creamy Cocktail Sauce, *188,* 189
    Southern, and Cauliflower Grits, 62, *63*
Smoothies
    Banana Blueberry Meal Replacement, 55
    Creamy Peach-Orange Smoothie, 51
    Sangria, 50
    Strawberry Shortcake, 52, *53*
    Tropical Greens, 50
S'mores for Me Dip, 224
Soups
    Cabbage, The Best-Ever, 126
    Chicken Pot Pie, 87
    Creamy Beet Bisque, 78
    Easy Chicken Ramen, *192,* 193–94
    Italian Wedding, *88,* 89
    Lemon-Dill Chicken, Greek, *76,* 77
    Pumpkin Bisque, 82, *83*
    Salmon Chowder, 79
Sour cream
    Thousand Island Dressing, 144
    Tzatziki Sauce, *164,* 165
Souvlaki, Deconstructed Pork, with Tzatziki Sauce, *164,* 165
Spinach
    Blueberry Kale Spring Green Salad, 98, *99*
    Coconut Red Lentil Dal with, 124, *125*

Easy Egg Bite Casserole, 201
Italian Wedding Soup, *88,* 89
Sweet Potato Frittata, *70,* 71
Tropical Greens, 50
Spirulina powder
    Tropical Greens, 50
Squash
    Beefy Enchilada Skillet, 210, *211*
    electric pressure cooker cook times, 21
    Pepperoni Pizza, 141
    Pumpkin Bisque, 82, *83*
    Spaghetti, Lasagna Casserole, 203–4
    Summertime Veggie Salad with Lemon Tahini Dressing, 96, *97*
Sriracha Mayo, 196
Stand/hand mixer, 44
Starch portion sizes, 6
Stews
    Ginger-Turmeric Chicken, 80–81
    Mango and Black Bean, Caribbean, 86
Strawberry(ies)
    Mini Maple Vanilla Nut Cakes, *216,* 217
    Shortcake Smoothie, 52, *53*
Strip Sauce, 177
Sustainably sourced, defined, 40
Sweeteners, 37
Sweet Potato(es)
    Bang Bang Chicken, *148,* 149
    Caribbean Mango and Black Bean Stew, 86
    Frittata, *70, 71*

Summertime Veggie Salad with Lemon Tahini Dressing, 96, *97*

T
Taco Chicken, 176
Tacos
    Cauliflower Tinga, 202
    Ground Tofu, 134, *135*
    Hamburger, *212,* 213
Taco Seasoning, 234, *235*
Tahini
    Easy Three-Ingredient, 239
    Honey Harissa Carrots, 114, *115*
    Lemon-Dill, and Paprika Vinaigrette, Roasted Eggplant with, *122,* 123
    Lemon Dressing, Summertime Veggie Salad with, 96, *97*
Teriyaki Salmon Rice Bowls, 146, *147*
Teriyaki Sauce, 146
Thousand Island Dressing, 144
Thyroid disease, 6–7
Time management, 8
Tofu
    Ground, Tacos, 134, *135*
    Spaghetti Squash Lasagna Casserole, 203–4
Tomatoes
    Jollof Rice with Red Beans, 130
    Mediterranean Herb and Bean Salad, 94
    Tangy Barbecue Sauce, 241
Tortillas
    Air-Fryer Mini Pepperoni Pizza, 171
    Bean and Rice Burritos, 137

Beefy Enchilada Skillet, 210, *211*
Buffalo Chicken Wraps, 176
Cauliflower Tinga Tacos, 202
Chicken Enchilada Roll-Ups, 182
Green Chile Chicken Enchiladas, 200
Ground Tofu Tacos, 134, *135*
Hamburger Tacos, *212,* 213
Red Chile Tostada, 140
Sheet Pan Fajitas, 208, *209*
Tostada, Red Chile, 140
Tres Leches, Dairy-Free, *228,* 229
Tuna
    Melts, Classic, *178,* 179
    Pasta Salad, 186, *187*
    Salad, 13
Turkey
    Chili, 3-Bean, 160
    Parm Meatloaf Minis, 161
    Reuben, Lightened-Up, 144, *145*
Turmeric-Ginger Chicken Stew, 80–81
Tzatziki Sauce, *164,* 165

V

Vegetable(s). See also specific vegetables
Broth, 244
Curry Chicken Stir-Fry, 172, *173*
electric pressure cooker cook times, 22
organic/conventionally grown/raised, 38–41
Platter with Ranch, 13
portion sizes, 6
Rice Pilaf, 108, *109*
Simple Salad, 14
Summertime Veggie Salad with Lemon Tahini Dressing, 96, *97*

W

Walnuts
Blueberry Kale Spring Green Salad, 98, *99*
Carrot Cake with Cashew Cream Frosting, 220–22, *221*
Mini Maple Vanilla Nut Cakes, *216,* 217

Z

Zucchini
Beefy Enchilada Skillet, 210, *211*
Pepperoni Pizza, 141
Summertime Veggie Salad with Lemon Tahini Dressing, 96, *97*